enjoy
Love,
Di

THE SQUIRREL CAGE

The
Squirrel
Cage

THE BEST OF DOUGLASS WELCH

Edited by Ruth Welch

Illustrations by Bob McCausland

MADRONA PUBLISHERS, INC.   •   SEATTLE

Library of Congress Cataloging in Publication Data

Welch, Douglass.
  The squirrel cage.

  I. McCausland, Bob. II. Title.
PZ3.W4424Sq   [PS3545.E498]   813'.5'4   76-45418
ISBN 0-914842-15-3 pbk.

Madrona Publishers, Inc.
113 Madrona Place East
Seattle, Washington 98112

Foreword

Douglass Welch was born in Boston and grew up in Tacoma, Washington, where his father, Charles B. Welch, was managing editor of the *Tacoma News-Tribune*. At the age of fifteen, Douglass started his newspaper career on that paper as a summertime cub reporter. After graduating from the University of Washington, he joined the editorial staff of the *Cleveland Plain Dealer*, returning to Seattle later as a reporter and feature writer for the *Seattle Times*, and subsequently for the *Seattle Post-Intelligencer*. In addition to his newspaper work, he wrote short pieces of humor for the *Saturday Evening Post*, where his "Mr. Digby" stories became a steady feature for years and were later published in book form. A number of his stories were adapted for films, radio and television, and many of his short pieces and stories were included in anthologies and collections.

After winning the Hearst Newspapers Award for humorous news reporting for two successive years, Douglass was assigned to write a daily column for King Features Syndicate, and "The Squirrel Cage" column was born. Since his death in 1968 there have been many requests for a collection of columns, and this book is the response.

My gratitude goes first to the readers of "The Squirrel Cage" who have encouraged me to persevere; to Morris J.

Alhadeff, whose support and assistance never faltered; to Guy Williams, Mel Anderson, and Paul Soelberg, who contributed invaluable advice; and to Dan Levant, whose appreciation of Doug's humor led him to publish this book.

RUTH WELCH (Green Eyes)

Contents

THE SQUIRREL CAGE

CHAPTER I

The Widow

Like I keep telling you, I live in this peculiar neighborhood and it is getting more peculiar all the time. We have the fellow who already has everything so his wife gave him a cannon for Christmas, a real cannon which he fires from time to time and people say to each other, "It's the bomb." And we have the lady who puts on her old Girl Scout uniform and steps out on her patio and blows the bugle whenever something bugs her. And we have the old lady up the street who complains to the State Department that the Russians are pumping poison gas into her bedroom window, and they are, too. And we have the St. Bernard who makes martinis, but not very good ones, and nobody tells him because it would hurt his feelings. And we have Joe Oedipus, the psychiatrist's cat whose mother Won't Let Him Go. And we have Mrs. Dibble who throws sticks in the water for her husband to retrieve. And we have Tuppin, the cat next door, who turns the television on and off and chooses the programs for his family to look at and whose taste is superior to theirs. Well, now we have a new added attraction, we have a widow and she scares the women.

She moved in a couple of months ago, and all we saw of her at first was walking around in her yard in loose caftans. She seemed to have an inexhaustible supply of them, and they all had one thing in common beside their shapelessness.

3

They looked as if she had run them up out of living room draperies. The women of the neighborhood all liked her at first. Only Green Eyes, my wife, was suspicious. "I think she is concealing something with those caftans," she said.

Pretty soon some ladies got to know her enough to ask her why she always wore caftans. She said she loved to sew but she had never mastered anything harder than a caftan. Then we menfolk got to know her when she was trying to move a big rock in her yard. "I do believe the widow is trying to move a big rock," I said to a group of fellows, and we all went over to help her. Green Eyes called after us, "I don't think she has the slightest interest in where the rock is," and this turned out to be true. After we had moved the rock, the widow confessed she liked it better where it had been at first, and we moved it back. Then she brought out drinks and we talked about Life, and the widow turned out to be terribly intelligent because she agreed with everyone.

And then last week she suddenly appeared dressed up to go to town, and there should be a law against caftans because when you put one on her kind of figure it is like littering a national park and despoiling scenery which belongs to everyone. And we cried out, "How about that!" and "Hey, hey, Jack!" and like that. But she is not going to get any more rocks moved for her. Some of us are not even allowed to walk anymore on her side of the street.

When a common danger threatens, wives fly to one another's assistance and form a Common Front. I guess that's what must have happened the other day when I was painting the back fence, out of sight of the house and Green Eyes. The Widow came along and began to help me. Actually she isn't a widow. She is more like divorced a couple of times, but "widow" is easier to say than "divorcee," so the fellows around the neighborhood call her The Widow.

I don't know what the wives call her. They don't understand her very well. She lives in the Monterey colonial down the street and drives a convertible that has four carburetors

and six straight pipes and is in mint condition. She is a very friendly girl with what you might call an eye-bugging figure. Her last husband, whoever he was, must have been out of his head to let her go because just watching her walk down the street is more refreshing than a weekend in the country.

The thing most of us fellows like about her is that she has no feminine guile. She's not predatory. She wants to be a pal to everybody. If she sees you working in your yard, she'll come up the street to talk to you.

I'm painting the fence on the alley side and The Widow comes along in denim shorts and blouse and says she loves to paint and would I mind if she helped me? Well, of course, what do you say? I said if she really liked it, please be my guest and take a brush. She painted pretty good, too, although my own painting slowed down a bit because I had to watch her and guide her how to paint into the corners.

The woman in the house across the alley suddenly comes out and asks me if I would mind looking at her washing machine which she says is making a funny noise. So I excuse myself and go down to this lady's basement and I listen to her washing machine, and I'm darned if I can hear any funny noise. It's washing clothes like mad.

And then she asks me how my wife is, which is a crazy question because she is in and out of our house every nine minutes to talk to Green Eyes and knows how she is better than I do. "I think I will run up and have a cup of coffee with your dear wife," she says, and I say, "I believe at the moment she is down at the supermarket trying to find a little hog liver for my lunch." And this lady says, "That's what I figured." It was kind of weird. If she already knew Green Eyes was away shopping, why did she say she was going up for a cup of coffee? Women are unfathomable.

Well, by the time I get back to the fence The Widow has finished a whole section, and she was telling me how much more handsome I look now that I have lost thirty pounds, and all of a sudden a woman from two houses down the alley wants me to look at her car. She can't get it started. I don't know why she came to me. I don't know much about cars. She's got a grown son who can take a car completely apart in forty minutes, and frequently does when the cops are busy at the other end of town. And this kid is sitting right on the patio! But she wants me to fix it, so I go down to look at it, and I find out the reason she can't start it is that someone has detached the battery cable!

Well, I am no sooner back with The Widow, who has finished another section, than a third wife comes up the alley with a plant for my wife which I must spade into the flower bed immediately. I never did get to finish talking about investments to The Widow.

So I went into the house finally and said to Green Eyes, "Guess what? The Widow helped me paint the fence this morning." And she said, "I know. I've been getting reports. There has been a general mobilization."

*   *   *

We've got bad trouble in our neighborhood at the moment with The Widow. For instance, Mrs. McMurty, who measures 40-40-40 straight up and down, threw all Mr. McMurty's clothes out of a second-story window onto the front lawn a few days ago because he was giving The Widow rides to and from downtown.

You see, The Widow is doing this work for charity, and she doesn't like to drive her car downtown and park it all day long, so she is taking the bus. She was standing there at the corner the other day when Mr. McMurty's car pool came along. Of course Mr. McMurty stopped and invited her in. It was the only gentlemanly thing to do. And then the other fellows were hollering at him, too. They were saying things like, "Gee, there is The Widow! Leave us pick her up," and "She can sit beside me!" And like that.

Usually Mr. McMurty's car pool just sits there silently

and in terror over the way Mr. McMurty drives. He is a retired banker and he only goes downtown to keep his hand in and foreclose a mortgage or two. I am told that he drives pretty casually and it is his theory that nobody would dare run into a banker. He pays no attention to traffic lights, either, because he regards them as only another attempt on the part of a bunch of socialists down at city hall to regiment the rugged individualism which made this country great.

So Mr. McMurty picked up The Widow and she sat on Mr. Dibble's lap, and the other fellows were saying, "Tomorrow is my turn," and like that, and The Widow said, "Oh, you silly boys." But the ride was what you might call animated. Everyone had a great time.

Mr. Dibble is not the world's greatest boob, but he will do until the world's greatest boob comes along. He went home and told Mrs. Dibble that The Widow had ridden on his lap, and right away Mrs. Dibble decided to let him have the car again to go to work in.

Also Mrs. Dibble called up Mrs. McMurty. And Mrs. McMurty went into executive session and tried her husband in absentia and found him guilty and sentenced him to exile. It took three of us most of the evening to get her even to open up the front door so we could plead his cause. She somehow got it in her head that The Widow had sat on Mr. McMurty's lap while he was driving, but we proved to her that Mr. McMurty's stomach hangs out so far it is all he can do to get it behind the steering wheel. So she let him back on probation.

So then Mr. Dibble was coming home one evening in his own car, and he saw The Widow at the bus stop downtown, and he impulsively stopped and let her in.

On the way home he stopped for a traffic light alongside our neighborhood bus, and he took his glasses off and started to clean them. And she said, "Oh, let me do that for you," and she cleaned them on the hem of her slip. Mr. Dibble said she was very ladylike and feminine and natural about it, and that the slip was trimmed with lots of lace.

Unhappily, Mrs. McMurty was on the bus and saw the whole thing and went into shock. When she recovered she called Mrs. Dibble.

Normally Mrs. Dibble treats her husband pretty mean. But she handled this report in an unpredictable way. She was nice to him and has been nice to him every since. He says it is like a second honeymoon. But Mrs. McMurty went home and had a terrible fight with Mr. McMurty again, just as if The Widow had cleaned *his* glasses on her slip.

I do feel it is an uphill job all the way being an attractive single woman in our neighborhood, and that everyone misunderstands her. Green Eyes says the trouble is that all the women *do* understand her.

*   *   *

I hear there are lots of people who jog, people who get out and run around a little bit every day in sweatsuits, and it does them so much Good, and also it is terribly fashionable and chic.

It started in my neighborhood with Mr. Fuller. His wife talked him into it. She said he was drinking too much beer (which was an understatement). So he began getting up a couple of hours earlier in the morning and jogging a mile with a can of beer in each back pocket. He opens up the first can and drinks it when he has gone past Father Ryan's church, and he drinks the second can on the way back, near the Dibbles' house.

Then, Dibble and young Mr. Starbright began to jog with Mr. Fuller (but they hate to stand around while he drinks his two cans of beer), and then Blair joined them three days a week, and *then* The Widow asked if *she* could go along!

She asked Mr. Dibble, and it never occurred to him that the wives of the joggers would care one way or another whether she went along. "Why sure, Lola," Mr. Dibble said. "We would love to have you. We will run by your house and pick you up at 7 A.M."

The first morning the group formed near Fuller's house and then jogged over to The Widow's and she came out in a jogging suit and jogged right along with them. Only her suit was a little tighter than the fellows' were, and looked a good deal more interesting.

Green Eyes got me out of bed. "Come quick and look out the window," she said. "All hell is loose this morning. The Widow is jogging with the joggers," and I had my nose pressed to the glass when the joggers came back fifteen minutes later and dropped The Widow off at her house.

I went down to breakfast in my bathrobe, and Green Eyes had the big coffee machine out. "What's with the coffee urn?" I asked, and she said: "I will probably pour anywhere up to thirty cups of coffee in another hour or two." And I said: "You got some kind of a meeting at *this* hour?" And she said: "No, but I know that the wives will all be over here talking about the joggers and The Widow."

And I said: "Well, it all seems innocent enough to me." And she said: "Ha!"

Mrs. Dibble was the first to arrive. She stopped after she drove her kids to school. She was shouting even before we got our front door open. "I guess you heard what *that woman* is doing *now*?" And Green Eyes said: "Yes, I saw her running with them this morning." And Mrs. Dibble said: "My husband has jogged his last jog, and that's the end of it!"

Green Eyes said: "Oh, I don't think it is that bad." And I said: "The Widow is only being sisterly again," and Mrs. Dibble said: "You stay out of this! What do you know about *anything*?" And I said: "Well, I know one thing. There certainly isn't anything very sexy about a woman getting out in a jogging suit and running along with a bunch of men." And Mrs. Dibble asked: "Does he have to sit here in the kitchen and listen to us talk? Can't you make him eat his breakfast somewhere else in the house?"

Green Eyes told me: "Now, honey, you can stay and

finish your breakfast if you don't say anything. This is woman-talk and you don't understand it." The doorbell rang, and it was Mrs. Fuller and Mrs. Blair, and Mrs. Cooper. Mr. Cooper was jogging that morning, too.

"What nauseates *me*," Mrs. Fuller said, "is that The Widow is so healthy-looking. I always tell my husband, look out for the *healthy* types." And Mrs. Cooper said: "She came running by *our* house with the whole pack behind her, and her cheeks were flushed and her hair was streaming out, and she was the picture of health and spirit, and I wanted to throw up."

And I said: "Well, the answer is obvious. Some of the rest of you ladies have got to jog, too." And Mrs. Dibble said in a fury: "*Decent* women have something else to do at that hour. They are cooking *their husbands'* breakfasts and making school lunches or getting dressed to go to work while their husbands are out *flirting*."

* * *

The ladies are trying to marry The Widow off to young Mr. Starbright. He's the widower who has two or three small boys. I don't know whether it is two or three. They sound like five when they are playing in the alley behind my house. They have wagons and they pretend they are racing cars and that they are revving up the motors, and they make a nasty juicy noise. I went out the other day and said to one of them, "Why can't you make believe you have a new *silent* jet motor?" and the kid said coldly: "That wouldn't be no fun." And I said: "When I was a boy, we boys used to pretend to hunt Indians and we were very quiet so the Indians wouldn't know where we were." And the kid said: "Oh, boy, let's kill pushers!" and they went down to the drug store and got nine dollars' worth of caps, and it sounded like World War II for three days.

I suppose I could ask Mrs. Fuller how many kids Starbright has. She is running in and out of his house like a revolving door — with fresh home-baked bread and puddings and birthday presents and I don't know what. Starbright has a housekeeper who comes in at noon and cleans up and gets dinner started and watches the boys until he comes home, but the women around here think she lacks "a mother's touch."

Mrs. McMurty is always running down there, too, and she knows the contents of young Starbright's refrigerator better than he does. Mrs. McMurty and Mrs. Blair do all his shopping for him and his menu planning, and Green Eyes hauls the kids out to the zoo once in a while or has them in for lunch on school holidays when I am upstairs trying to write some of my most beautiful prose.

Sometimes when Starbright comes home he finds the housekeeper and Mrs. Blair and Mrs. McMurty and Mrs. Fuller and Green Eyes all monkey-grabbing around, and he serves them a martini and they think it is deliciously wicked to be having a cocktail in a bachelor's diggings with two, three, maybe five noisy kids around, breaking the place up.

I will say none of us husbands worries about his wife being at Starbright's because he is as good as he is handsome, and he ought to be in a museum somewhere because he is so decent he is rare. He doesn't have much drive, I guess, and the wives all say what he needs is a Good Woman, and they think the Good Woman ought to be The Widow.

As soon as Starbright moved into the neighborhood, why there was a succession of elaborate parties to which Starbright and The Widow were invited, and I doubt he knew what the neighborhood wives had planned for him, but she caught it right away.

It seems to me that she is not the least bit interested in Starbright. But Green Eyes tells me that when a woman shows no interest whatever in a fellow, that means for sure she is plenty interested. I don't understand women and this doesn't make any sense to me at all. On the other hand, I have never known my wife to be wrong in matters of this sort.

For one thing, she points out, while The Widow does not

talk much to young Starbright at neighborhood parties, she does encourage his boys to come around to her house and she gives them cookies and lets them watch her television and she sometimes takes them down to the village for ice cream or to the park for a picnic. Green Eyes says this is terribly and subtly significant, even though she always returns them home well before their father is scheduled to show up. I don't think it is so significant.

I think I know how The Widow feels about Starbright. She feels like I do. At the Fullers' married daughter's baby shower last Thursday night somebody offered him a drink, and he said: "Oh, no. I have already had *two!*" And somebody said: "But that is just a warm-up. Now the real serious cross-country drinking *begins.*" And The Widow said: "I don't think you should *ply* him. Thank heaven, we have one decent, upright man in this otherwise depraved community." But she didn't sound sincere.

Now I don't want you to think that she is the type who wants the menfolk walking around on the ceiling, or that she lushes it up herself. She is very ladylike about her drinking. She accepts anything you hand her when a party starts steaming up. But, like my own wife, she doesn't drink it. She puts it unobtrusively aside when nobody is looking. Behind the sofa, or something. Sometimes she pours her drink into some fellow's drink when his head is turned, and he goes home in a wheelbarrow wondering where he miscounted.

I guess you think it is strange that men go to baby showers in our neighborhood and that there is drinking, but there are a number of babies and grandbabies being born around here lately, and our wives were going out two, three nights a week, and we finally insisted on being included. Anything to get away from this season's television.

One day The Widow pinch hit as den mother for the Cub Scout troop the Starbright boys belong to. Mrs. McMurty was pretty sore about this. She said the Boy Scouts were certainly letting down the bars if they permitted a divorced woman who never had any children to become a den mother. She called up the Boy Scouts and made a big beef, but Green Eyes heard about it and called up the Boy Scouts and said The Widow was a wonderful woman, really.

I understand the Boy Scouts sent out a lady to talk to The Widow, and the lady was charmed by her and stayed for the cub meeting. The Widow played baseball with the boys in the back yard. Mr. McMurty came out to make some more pictures of her leaping around, and Mrs. McMurty threw up a second-story window and shouted at him: "What do you think you are doing *now*, you old goat?" Mrs. McMurty at the moment was dressed in her husband's old pants and hunting jacket, and *that* finished *her* with the Boy Scout lady.

Last week the housekeeper left early and asked Mrs. Fuller to drop by and look at the Beef Burgundy she had started for the Starbright dinner. Mrs. Fuller added a little curry to it, and then Mrs. McMurty came by and added bay leaves and allspice and Mrs. Blair stirred in some nutmeg. Green Eyes went down and added more wine, and my mother-in-law followed her with some dumpling dough. My mother-in-law makes the world's lightest and largest dumplings, delicate as a baby's breath, but they are deceiving. I think they still keep rising in the stomach because it is like somebody blew you up with a bicycle pump.

Well, Starbright and the boys worked their way down to the bottom of the pot and did the dishes and then collapsed in front of television, and at ten o'clock when Mrs. Fuller came in to find out how they liked the Beef Burgundy, they were all soundly asleep.

Green Eyes points out that all three of The Widow's former husbands were dreadfully nice and thoroughly decent, and when she gets ready to marry again, it will probably be to exactly the same type. Green Eyes is not worried about The Widow wooing *me* away. And I say: "Why not? I am a decent fellow and I *can* be nice when I put my mind to it." And she says: "You sit and watch television in your undershirt and scratch your stomach through the most beautiful parts." And I say: "But how would The Widow know *that*?" And she says: "Because I told her."

CHAPTER II

The Cannoneer

I told you about this fellow, Mr. Jack, who has a cannon out on his patio pointed at the second-story bathroom window of his neighbor next door. I gave him a cannonball for his birthday, and he almost went out of his mind wondering what it would be like to put a real cannonball through somebody's bathroom while it was occupied. I didn't dream he would want to fire the cannonball. I intended it for decoration only. I didn't realize he would want to fire it until his wife told me later that she has to keep it hidden. She lets him have the cannonball to play with from time to time, but she stands right by to restrain him if temptation overcomes him. She is not at all pleased that I gave it to him.

The situation is touchy at the moment. There may be a lawsuit. The neighbor has consulted an attorney. But it doesn't seem to be against any law to *point* a cannon at someone's bathroom window. You can only go to court if someone *threatens* to fire a cannonball through your bathroom or does actually *fire* such a cannonball. In the latter eventuality, of course, after the cannonball has been fired it is too late to go to court to stop it.

This neighbor, Mr. Fuller, asserts that the cannon pointed at his bathroom has, in effect, deprived him of the use of his bathroom because no member of his family cares to tarry there. They just rush in and out. And they won't use it unless some other member of the family is standing guard at a bedroom window watching the patio and calling out at intervals, 'It's okay, so far.'

The other night at the Community Club meeting the neighbor said, "We all use the downstairs bathroom now because there is, I think, a real and dreadful possibility that this kook will have five martinis some night. Then he will find the cannonball his wife hides from him. And then somebody in my family will go into my upstairs bathroom and turn on the light and bang, wham, that's it, brother!"

When she bought this cannon, Mrs. Jack went into a ship chandler's and said, "I wish to buy a cannon for my husband." And they said, "What kind of a cannon?" And she said, "Any kind of a cannon that makes a big loud noise because he loves big noises." And they said, "Well, here is a Lyle gun from the Coast Guard. It is used to shoot lines in sea rescues. But it could also be used as a saluting cannon." And she said, "Fine. Have it gift-wrapped and be a prince and put it in the trunk of my car."

And they said, "Lady, with the wheels and carriage this weighs pretty near 450 pounds. Your rear fenders would be right down on the tires." So they sent it out on a truck Christmas Eve and four men set it down on the patio, and ever since, Mr. Jack has been counting the days until he can fire it again. New Year's Eve is about all. But he does often go out and wheel it around and make the motions of filling the barrel with powder and ball, and he says, "Bang!" and "Bulls Eye!" and things like that. There's just so much frustration a red-blooded man can take so he joined a cannon-owners' society. They call it a cannonade. They all have cannons, and they wear caps with crossed cannon emblems and they have blazers, but the best thing they have is a place to shoot their cannons.

This place is an old quarry where the sound is magnified and echoes and re-echoes something fierce. Most of the fellow members leave their cannons locked up in the old quarry motor shed, and winch them out to the firing line just about the time that church takes up a quarter of a mile down the road. They have an arrangement with the preacher where he rings the bell in the church tower when service is concluded. The bell rings and immediately the countryside sounds like World War II.

The first time they got together in the quarry they didn't know about the church service, and the minister was telling his congregation that the enemy was drawing near. "He is coming down the road," he said, and he pointed dramatically toward the window. Of course, what he meant by the enemy was The Devil and Booze and Gin Rummy and like that. A few seconds later Mr. Jack shot his one-pounder, and the president of the cannonade shot his old French 75, and six other cannons went off, and the minister paled and said, "It is later than I thought."

Mr. Jack does not like to leave his cannon at the quarry because he says you never know when the Democrats might rise and he needs it at home. So he got this jeep and trailer, and he winches his cannon up on his trailer from his patio and ties it down securely and then goes out on the freeway with the cannon pointed at the car behind him. Almost everybody passes Mr. Jack on these occasions. Or drops way back.

The first time he drove to the quarry Mr. Jack wasn't sure whether his Jeep and trailer qualified as a truck or not, and he drove into the state weighing station and the fellow looked out the window and said, "What have you got there, Clyde?" And Mr. Jack said, "A cannon," and the fellow said, "I can see it is a cannon. What do you figure on doing with it?"

And Mr. Jack wouldn't tell him. He said, "I believe that the only matter at issue here is whether or not my Jeep and trailer and cannon constitute commercial carriage and are subject to state commercial wheel-loading regulations." And the fellow at the window said to another officer, "I think you had better go out and talk to this joker, Harry, because it sounds to me like he is walking on the ceiling."

So the other officer came out and said, "Where did you get this here cannon?" And Mr. Jack said, "My wife gave it to

me for Christmas." And the officer said, "Okay, wise guy. Just pull over there and stand until you can give me a civil answer."

What sprung Mr. Jack were two other cannoneers who went by and recognized his Jeep and trailer in the weighing station. For a while their three cannons were trained on both officers. But they worked it out. One of the cannoneers is a lawyer specializing in cannons, and he said there is absolutely no law which says (1) that a cannon has to go through a weighing station, and (2) that cannons cannot be freely wheeled about the countryside — even loaded with powder and ball and a sputtering fuse.

When the officers were relieved that afternoon they came down to the quarry and Mr. Jack and the others let them fire two or three rounds each. Now they are great friends, and when the hobby-artillery moves down the highway every Sunday afternoon everybody waves at the weighing station.

Well, there was a cocktail party in the neighborhood and another fellow who owns a cannon told Mr. Jack, "I do believe that the bore of your cannon will precisely allow the introduction of a can of beer, and I further believe that if you experiment with the charges of powder you use, you will very soon be able to drop a can of beer anywhere in the neighborhood that you want it."

And Mr. Jack said, "But the cannon heats up and the beer would get hot." And this other fellow said, "The secret is to freeze the can solid in the deepfreeze. It then arrives on the target at exactly the right temperature."

Mr. Jack looked like a minor prophet who has just experienced a major revelation.

The next Sunday Mr. Jack beckoned Mr. Fuller over to his patio and said, "Leave us see if I can shoot a can of cold beer over to that chair where you were sitting." And Mr. Fuller said, "I just don't like it already." And Mr. Jack said, "I believe I can use just enough powder to make a little puff and scarcely any noise and put a can practically in your lap." And Mr. Fuller said, "And then what?" And Mr. Jack said, "The beer is yours to drink." And Mr. Fuller said, "I like it."

The first can cleared the alley but fell short of Mr. Fuller's chair. There was relatively little noise, no worse than a backfire. The next shot put the can right at Mr. Fuller's feet. Mr. Jack shot twelve cans in all, or two six-packs, and Mr. Fuller got loaded to the eyeballs and behaved rather badly at dinner. What happened actually, was that he fell into the pot roast while he was carving it.

Mrs. Fuller had a talk with Mrs. Jack and the Great Beer Can War seems at an end.

* * *

Last Sunday Mr. Jack shot some canned beer over into the Fullers' yard again. He has the technique down beautifully now. He knows within a quarter of an ounce how much black powder he needs to put a can down exactly at Mr. Fuller's feet when Mr. Fuller is sitting expectantly on his patio. Of course, the occasional can will roll a little, but Mr. Fuller does not seem to mind getting up and chasing it. The deal is that any beer shot over is Mr. Fuller's to dispose of. And mostly he disposes of it by drinking it.

The first can Mr. Jack shot, why he forgot he had already put in one bag of powder and he added a second. The can went clean over Mr. Fuller's house and dropped across the street at the feet of Mr. Kilkenny who was mowing his lawn. Mr. Kilkenny cried out, "Manna from heaven!" and stopped mowing his lawn and followed the trajectory of the beer toward Mr. Jack's cannon. He was passing through Mr. Fuller's backyard and Mr. Fuller said: "Pull up a chair. This is going to be an interesting and profitable afternoon."

Mr. Kilkenny never did finish his lawn. Mrs. Kilkenny called him several times, but he wouldn't come, and she investigated, and I am afraid she denounced her husband in front of Mr. Fuller — and in front of a number of other fellows who had gathered by this time. Mr. Kilkenny suggested that she rout out their high school son who was watching television and direct *him* to finish the lawn. But she wouldn't do it because the boy is delicate, so she finished the lawn herself.

It may have been Mrs. Kilkenny who called the police, I don't know. Or it may have been Mrs. McMurty who was sore because Mr. McMurty was at the Fullers', too. Anyway, our friendly neighborhood prowl car came around and they watched Mr. Jack firing his cannon, and they conceded that it made a good deal less noise than all the power lawnmowers and the edgers the wives were running at the moment.

Actually the wives were not so disturbed over the fact that Mr. Jack was shooting beer again as they were over the fact that he was shooting 8 per cent ale. He shot five six-packs, which doesn't sound like much, but this stuff is dreadfully potent.

The wives all call it "killer beer" because it disorganizes a husband faster even than a double martini. I mean, after two cans you are sitting there with a bird on your head.

Except for the fact that everyone in Mr. Fuller's yard got loaded and began hollering for Mrs. Fuller to bring out something to eat (which she wouldn't do at first), it was an eminently proper gathering. The prowl car boys came back when they were off shift, and they lent a lot of dignity to the occasion.

Well, the wives telephoned each other and decided to pool their Sunday dinners and bring them over to the Fullers' yard, and the cops called up their wives to hustle over, and pretty soon there were about fifty people in the Fullers' yard, kids and everything. And the wives had like a buffet, and plenty of strong black coffee.

But hours after he had eaten, Mr. Dibble went back to his home and stepped through the ceiling from the open attic while he was finishing a wiring job. His leg came down into his mother-in-law's room, and she screamed for her daughter. "Come and see what that stupid husband of yours has done to my house!" she cried.

And Mr. McMurty put his car away and went a little too far into the garage — right through the partition into the utility room and Mrs. McMurty's washing, in fact. And Mr. Blair dropped Mrs. Blair's silver coffee urn in the street bringing it home, and stepped on the lid, and Mrs. Blair said some very ugly things. And Mrs. Fuller insisted that Mr. Fuller get down on his hands and knees and clean up the yard, which he did way past midnight.

There is nothing like a quiet, restful, bucolic Sunday to restore a fellow's spirit and to put him in fighting shape to hit the job again on Monday.

CHAPTER III

The Fullers

Mr. Fuller, my neighbor, moves his lips when he reads. He is about six weeks into a speed-reading course, and he still moves his lips, and that's the big trouble. His lips can't keep up with his eyes. His eyes will finish a page in a moment but his lips are still struggling with the first two sentences.

His teacher will say to him: "Mr. Fuller, you can never be a speed-reader as long as you insist on forming the sound of each word on your lips because your mouth and lips can't articulate as quickly as your eyes can absorb. And also it is against the rules to bring canned beer to class."

Mr. Fuller said: "Nobody knows I have a can of beer except you. I always sit in the back." And she said: "Well, it is very distracting to try to teach a speed-reading class and see a can of beer raised to a mouth in the back of the room."

He said: "Beer helps me to think." It does, too. I remember one Sunday I went over to his patio to ask him about a stock. He had been sitting there all afternoon, and I counted seven empties beside his chair. I showed him an annual statement to stockholders and I said: "You know, these people owe a hundred million dollars which they must soon begin to pay off at the rate of five million a year. Are they going to be able to do it, or will they have to be refinanced?"

He sat there, maybe five, ten minutes, reading slowly, lips

moving, right forefinger pointing out the words one at a time. "Yes," he said, "with that kind of cash flow, they can do it easily."

Mr. Fuller does very well on the stock market, and he is no dummy at real estate, either. I mean people see him pick up a document and form the words visibly as he reads, and they say, "Oh, boy, can I ever take this apple-knocker! He looks like he has been living up in a tree." But a couple of days after a deal, they find out.

It was Mrs. Fuller who signed him up for the speed-reading course. She told Green Eyes, "I suppose I have one of the nicest, kindest husbands a woman could ask for, and I know he is smart, too — in a business way. But I shall scream one of these days when he is reading a newspaper and moving his lips. The trouble is, he reads so slowly. He has to wait for his lips to catch up with his eyes."

Mr. Fuller didn't object when he discovered what his wife had done. He told me that he considers the things she does to be the natural hazards of being married. You can expect women to do impulsive, irrational things. The first lesson, he took along an insurance policy and quietly asked the teacher to read the fine print on the reverse side.

The young lady read both sides of the policy in less than a minute, and said, "It is as easily read as anything else. It is a policy on the furniture in your home. It also provides for liability protection and theft. Do you want me to state the principal amounts?"

And Mr. Fuller said slowly, "No. I just want you to tell me what it says about payment for damage or loss to the mortgagee rather than to the owner under certain conditions." And the teacher said, "That's a detail." And he said, "It just happens to be a little more important than a detail. It might mean the difference between living good on roast beef, or standing out in the cold without any pants on and the snow coming down." She said, "Well, this is specialized reading, and we do offer a graduate course in specialized reading, and

I will be happy to refer you to it when you have finished with your generalized speed reading."

Mr. Fuller said, "Oh, you needn't mind. I don't mind reading books and newspapers fast, but I think I will always read insurance policies and mortgages and debenture agreements very slowly, a word at a time."

She said, "Mr. Fuller, to get the most out of this kind of course, you must *believe*." And he said, "I will believe, except where money is involved."

Three weeks later he came home and picked up a book and read it in three minutes. Mrs. Fuller said, "That's marvelous! What did you get out of that book?"

And he said, "Well, there was a mouse that ran up a clock. There was some woman who rode to Banbury Cross with rings on her fingers and bells on her toes. And then there was some child named Wee Willie Winkie who ran through the town in a nightgown. The characters I remember, but the story is a little vague. It doesn't seem to hang together."

And Mrs. Fuller said: "Oh, for heaven's sake, you were reading Mother Goose. But for once your lips weren't moving!" A minute later he was reading the Wall Avenue Chronicle, however, and his lips were chewing every word and his finger was pointing them out.

*   *   *

I believe Mrs. Fuller is an excellent driver, but when she sits in her husband's car she is the worst back-seat driver I have ever heard. She doesn't *say* anything actually that you can reprimand her for. It's just that she covers up her eyes with her hands when he comes up to an intersection and like that. "For heaven's sake," he says, "why do you cover up your eyes?" And she says: "I don't want to see what is going to happen."

And she also goes "Eeeeeeeek!" You can't translate "Eeeeeeeek!" It could mean anything. Mostly she goes "Eeeeeeeek!" when he is overtaking another automobile on the freeway. But she will go "Eeeeeeeek!" even when he is passing a bicycle or a roadside fruit stand or an old woman waiting for the bus with a basket on her head.

In time, on a long drive, Mr. Fuller becomes furious, and tells her if she says "Eeeeeeeek!" once more he will let her out of the car and their marriage is at an end and he will move to the club. So she stops saying "Eeeeeeeek!" Now she draws in her breath sharply and pushes her feet hard against the floorboards. I can't write down the sound of drawing in breath abruptly, but it is the most frightening thing you ever heard. You expect a tiger to spring. You feel like the Metroliner is coming up the highway behind you.

Once the Fullers were driving Green Eyes and me to the country club and it was a beautiful day and a fine paved road, and he was going only about forty miles an hour and there wasn't a car in sight in any lane, and she drew in her breath sharply and pushed the floorboards, and I said, because I try to be helpful: "Psychologists say that when a wife expresses continued apprehension about her husband's driving, it is one indication that romance between them is waning." And Mrs. Fuller turned to me and said: "Who asked you?" And she said: "Big deal!" But I noticed she didn't push the floorboards again and she didn't draw in her breath.

* * *

Sex has reared its Ugly Head again among the young, and this time it picked the worst of all possible places — in the home of my neighbor, Mrs. Fuller. She is a nice lady and really rather liberal in all her thinking except about Sex. I mean, she has even scissored long passages out of the family Bible because she did not consider them fit for the eyes of the very young, or even the eyes of her husband, for that matter.

The family was eating dinner the other night and the Fullers' high-school-age daughter said: "Daddy, tell me all about social diseases and sex." And Mr. Fuller said: "Hahzat again?" And Mrs. Fuller said: "Now that will be enough of that! What a dreadful thing to bring up at the dinner table. What put *that* in your mind?"

The girl said: "We were talking about it in school today, and I've got to do a paper on it tonight." And her mother said: "I never heard of such a thing. What did they say about sex in school today, for heaven sake?" And she said: "Oh, we have this book, you know. It is called a social science manual but it is mostly about sex, and things like homosexuality and all that. . ." Mrs. Fuller rose right up straight from her chair and said: "I will call up that principal of yours first thing tomorrow morning and tell *him* a Thing or Two!"

And the daughter said: "Oh, Mama, don't be so old-fashioned! They will just think you are a square. Don't make a big thing about it or the other kids will laugh at me."

Mr. Fuller said: "Your mother believes that a girl should not know anything about sex until after she has been married and has had two or three children — and then it is safe to tell her." And Mrs. Fuller said: "You stay out of this! I think it is a mother's obligation to teach her children about sex, and it is certainly her right to decide at what age they should be told."

He said: "Okay. Go fight City Hall."

Mrs. Fuller called up Mrs. McMurty immediately. "Have you heard what they are teaching the children at our own Benedict Arnold High School?" she began. Mrs. McMurty said: "Ah, ha! Communism! I knew it. I just knew it." Mrs. Fuller said: "It's worse than that. They are teaching them about Sex!" And Mrs. McMurty said: "Oh, *that*. Are you sure they are not teaching them Communism, too?" Mrs. Fuller said: "It is entirely possible that the Communists are introducing sex education into the schools to undermine American Society."

Mrs. Fuller asked Mrs. McMurty if she would accompany her to a conference with the principal the next morning, and Mrs. McMurty said she would. "I think," Mrs. McMurty said, "if you dig deep enough you will find that Communism is behind all this. Or Democrats."

Mrs. Fuller came over here the next morning to have coffee with my wife and The Widow was already here. Mrs. Fuller asked Green Eyes if she would join a delegation, and Green Eyes said: "First tell me what it is all about." When Mrs. Fuller told her, she said: "Yes, I think I will go along to make sure the principal gets a fair hearing. It's quite possible, you know, that he has no choice in the matter, and it is also quite possible that this may be a Good Thing." Mrs. Fuller said: "Don't you think a mother should be the one to instruct children about sex?" And Green Eyes said: "Yes, but with some mothers it might be better that the children learn from school."

Well, Mrs. Fuller didn't want her to go along then, but Green Eyes insisted, and The Widow said she would go, too.

Mrs. Fuller said to The Widow: "What do you know about sex?" And she said: "I've had three husbands, haven't I? I should know *something*." And Mrs. Fuller said: "But you don't know anything about *children* and sex!" And The Widow said: "I was a child myself once. Wouldn't that qualify me?"

So there is a delegation going to the school tomorrow, and I'll bet there will be twenty women, most of them going only to hear what The Widow says to the principal. I understand the Fuller girl *did* write her paper for school. Mrs. Fuller found a false start in the wastebasket. The Fuller girl had written: "An awful lot is being made out of Sex these days, and I think young people do not think it is really all that important. You find sex in advertisements and in books and in movies and on the television but I really think sex is not such a big part of life except it is nice to be married and have children which is what nature intends. I do not care to discuss social diseases because a friend of my mother says they are Communistic. . . ."

* * *

I blame it all on Freud, actually. If he hadn't invented sex, there wouldn't be any sex to plague us today. This is not my original idea, it was advanced in the meeting by Mrs. Cooper. She got up and said are we for decent American education or are we going to line up with Dr. Freud, and a lot of parents shouted, "No, never!"

There was a lot of talk at the meeting about Freud, and finally Sam Freud, who runs the pants-pressing shop in the Village, got up and asked if people would please say "*Doctor* Freud" when they referred to Freud because he said some people were confusing him, Sam, with Dr. Freud, and it was bad for his pants-pressing business.

Mrs. Blair got up and said: "Sex is all right in its place, and I am not going to say a little sex instruction is harmful, but I would much rather have my children spell properly and read well and do arithmetic correctly than study social diseases and deviates. . . ."

Well, a couple of teachers got up and began hollering that this was *not fair*. Mrs. Cartwright said her Kenneth got very good grades at Benedict Arnold High but still spelled "cat" with two *t*'s. She said that Kenneth's roll-room teacher had prepared a notice to go out to the PTA and that Mrs. Carter found five misspelled simple words in it. I turned to Green Eyes and said: "Mrs. Cartwright has just made certain that her son Kenneth will be a dead stinking pigeon at Benedict Arnold High from this time on, no matter how hard he works."

CHAPTER IV

The McMurtys

A tip of my hat to Mrs. McMurty who lives across the street in our peculiar neighborhood. Mrs. McMurty is 40-40-40 straight up and down and is a compensatory eater because she feels nobody loves her, and she is austere and she hollers out the living room window when her husband talks to The Widow in the adjoining yard. But still there is a lot that is very admirable about Mrs. McMurty and I recognize her as the stuff which made America great. In another, earlier day she would have been shooting Indians from the ramparts or locking up sinners like you and me for the weekend in the stocks. She can freeze another woman at twenty paces with a single cold glance and her voice sometimes has an edge like a scythe, and she can use it much the same way, too.

She drives her automobile at a good steady twenty-five miles an hour whether she is on a country road or a freeway, and she sits there grim and straight-backed as if she were wheeling a juggernaut through the haunts and over the bodies of infidels. When the freeways opened, she single-handedly put traffic control back to wagon-train days. She would change lanes whenever she liked, without signaling, and ninety-five cars in three lanes behind her would snuggle against one another in a shattering crescendo of yielding sheet metal.

She invariably made for right-hand exits from the center lane suddenly, and she often got lost and just stopped until someone would give her directions. It got so that the fellows up in the helicopter who were broadcasting traffic conditions would recognize her car below them and would warn their listeners: "There is going to be trouble at 145th Street any minute now." And there always was. And Mrs. McMurty invariably got away unscathed. As far as the body repair shops in town were concerned, she was Miss Business Opportunity of the year.

But this year that is all changed now. She doesn't lose her way on freeways any more. She has devised a system. She hires a taxicab to drive ahead of her and show her the way on and off the ramps and what lane to stay in.

At first the taxicab companies thought she was kidding, but they know her well now. She picks up a cab at a predetermined spot near a freeway entrance, follows it in her own car at twenty-five miles an hour to the predetermined exit, and charges the cab to her husband and tips the driver handsomely. Never less than a dollar.

For weeks, Mr. McMurty, who is a retired banker and can be jolly about everything except money, couldn't understand how his wife could drive to their daughter's home and use both her own car and a taxicab. And he couldn't ask her because they don't talk much to each other.

Using a taxicab as a guide and an interference was an inspiration. The way this inspiration came, why Mrs. McMurty was confused on the freeway one day and she simply stopped her car straddling two lanes, and traffic backed up through three counties. Pretty soon a patrol car came along with lights flashing and siren going, and, of course, ambulances were already carrying people away two, three miles back.

So this young policeman got out and said, "What seems to be the trouble here?" and Mrs. McMurty said, "Don't take that tone of voice with me, young man! I don't know how to get off this freeway and I am lost, and I am going to sit here until somebody guides me to my destination."

Although she had broken sixty-eight laws, the officer looked at the set of her face and decided he wanted no part of messing with her. And he said, "All right, Lady, we will pull in front of you and you follow us carefully." And she said, "Not if you go faster than twenty-five." And he said, "Okay, Lady, twenty-five." So the patrol car preceded her for two miles with the siren going and took her down the off-ramp. Nine thousand people got home late that night.

Mrs. McMurty liked the idea of having an escort and the next time she called the first taxicab.

But today a police car has been parked in front of her house most of the afternoon, and I believe a police captain is inside Talking to Her for Her Own Good.

She got arrested yesterday on the freeway for going too slow. Also the taxicab she was following was stopped and its driver was arrested as well.

Mrs. McMurty may be 40-40-40 straight up and down (except when she wears her new $105 girdle) and she may be a monster, but she is also a Great Lady, and she does not brook insolence from civil servants, especially from police when, as everybody knows, they are heavily infiltrated by Democrats. "I do not know of any law," she said stiffly, "that sets a minimum speed on this Freeway," and the officer said: "No, but there is such a thing as driving to the common danger." He was trying to be nice to her because she reminded him of his grandmother.

Mrs. McMurty is a formidable sight in her seven-passenger Juggernaut and she handles it like a pilot bringing the Queen Elizabeth into her berth from the Hudson River. She invariably wears a large hat when she drives, and she wears it exactly level on her head, and the sight of the hat alone terrifies many oncoming and following motorists.

So she got arrested and McMurty told me the captain in charge of the city traffic squad called him up at the club where he was playing dominos. The captain said Mr. McMurty should have a good talk with his wife about venturing out on the Freeway, and Mr. McMurty told the captain: "I never talk to my wife about *anything* if I can help it." And the captain said: "But this is a serious situation, and conceivably some day she could go to jail." And McMurty said: "I will consider that a promise, and I am going to hold you to it."

Mrs. McMurty asked Green Eyes to come over and be a witness when the police arrived, but it wasn't necessary. It turned out to be a simply charming meeting. Very early in the conversation it developed that the captain is a Republican by birth, childhood training and natural tendency, and Mrs. McMurty warmed up to him immediately. She served him tea and a large slice of her wonderful chocolate Devil's Food cake which has marmalade and whipped cream and shaved-chocolate filling.

Green Eyes said the captain had the city traffic engineer prepare a special-marked map of the city for Mrs. McMurty showing her the shortest routes to and from the homes of her friends *not using the freeway*. Furthermore, a police car starting tomorrow will take her over these routes until she has become familiar with them, and she, on her part, has promised she will not go on the Freeway again. I believe this is inspired Modern Police Work, but I am afraid that it will mean that half of the city's automobile body repair shops will start laying off employees within a week or two.

* * *

Bankers seem to be seized at the moment by some kind of madness. I mean this bank credit-card business where they are actually making it possible for you to go out and burn your candle at both ends and spend your substance in riotous living.

I went into my own branch bank the other day to ask the manager to loan me a dollar for lunch because Green Eyes only lets me have ten dollars a week for everything. And when you are keeping a woman on the side, ten dollars does not go very far. Oh, actually I am not keeping a woman on the side; it's only when I see my married daughter from time to time, I buy her something pretty or some goody for the grandchildren, and then I am fresh out of lunch money for maybe weeks.

So I said to Mr. Pearce, he's my banker: "How are you fixed for a buck and a quarter?" And he said: "What is the quarter for?" And I said: "That's for pie." And he said: "Tell me where you can get a good piece of pie for a quarter these days, and I will go along with you." And I said: "I didn't say it was a *good* piece of pie. I only said it was a piece of pie."

And he said: "Is that the place where you found a fly in your soup?" And I said: "Yes, and when I called it to the waiter's attention, the waiter said: "Keep your voice down, or *everybody* around here will be wanting one!"

And Mr. Pearce said: "Frankly, Welch, although we

value your business, I do not think the money you have on deposit here compensates me for having to listen to your old beat-up comedy routines."

Well, he gave me the dollar and a quarter, and I don't have to pay it back until next week this time, and I don't have to pay interest on it because it came out of his own pocket, and I think this is banking in its finest flowering.

But then he said: "I notice that you haven't been using your bank credit card," and I said: "No, I haven't. As a matter of fact, I cut it up in little pieces and threw it away." And he said: "I don't think that was very gracious of you. Here we extend you credit and make it possible for you to walk into hundreds of shops and charge your purchases, and you repay our kindness by destroying the card."

And I said: "I kind of think of a bank as a father-figure, and I don't think a father-figure should be encouraging me to *spend* money. I think you should be encouraging me to *save*."

And he said, and I think this is terribly significant: "We banks don't think of ourselves anymore as father-figures. We like to think of ourselves as friendly big brothers, conducting you by your hot little hand through the perilous economic world of today."

I had an opportunity to discuss the bank credit-card situation that same night with Mr. McMurty. Although he is a retired banker, he is in and out of the old bank several times a day because they let him keep the key to the executive washroom and it is a great convenience as well as a signal honor.

McMurty's big interest now is his hobby — which is making pictures from his upstairs bedroom window of The Widow walking around in her yard next door. He has — I don't know how many — telescopic lenses, and he shoots The Widow through a part in the curtains. She always knows when he is taking pictures, though, because Mrs. McMurty opens the kitchen window and shouts at The Widow: "The old goat is upstairs making pictures of you again." And The

Widow always says: "I'm flattered," but I don't believe she is.

Anyway, McMurty got back about forty enlargements of The Widow and called me over to see them. He is selecting one to enter in the community Action Photo Exhibit at the Legion Hall next month, and he will call it "Eternal Woman." He won first prize last year on "Eternal Woman," and the year before on "Eternal Woman," both being The Widow. I guess nobody will ever forget that "Eternal Woman." It was The Widow in a bikini and a real swinger. And "Eternal Woman" the next year was The Widow mowing her own back lawn. Artistically it wasn't much, but the judges believed it set a good example for the other women of the neighborhood.

McMurty is an old-fashioned banker, and he said right off that he doesn't believe in credit cards for anybody, issued by anyone, and that he thinks money ought to be put in banks and that people ought not to be allowed to take it out to spend it on anything.

He also said he longed for the old days when tellers were elderly gentlemen in alpaca coats and were shackled behind their iron cages and lived on gruel. McMurty said the trouble with coddling depositors is that when a bank is nice to them, why pretty soon depositors begin to think that their money in the bank is really *theirs* and not the bank's.

But his heart really wasn't in it. He kept holding up pictures of The Widow and saying: "How about this!" and "Oh, Boy!" and "Hubba Hubba!" which are not strictly banking terms.

*   *   *

Starlings have been living on the roof of the McMurtys' house for, oh, two or three years now. It used to be a very pretty slate gray roof, and now it is a rather attractive white roof with bits of slate gray showing through.

Mrs. McMurty is out in front of her house again this morning in her husband's old trousers and hunting jacket and the hat with the fishhooks in it, and she is beating on a dishpan with a long wooden spoon. This used to send the starlings flying, but no more. Today the newcomers ask the old-timers: "Who is the monster beating the dishpan?" and the old-timers say: "It's the old broad who lives here, and boy, is she ever ding-a-ling!"

Mr. McMurty once borrowed a carbide cannon from an orchardist. This little gun operated automatically every thirty minutes and made a noise like a sonic boom. The starlings took off in a panic with each blast, and so did every neighbor within a three-block area. Mr. McMurty mounted the cannon on an empty fifty-barrel oil drum in the McMurty's back yard and he thought it was jolly fun, but the police made him stop the second day.

The noise affected birds other than the starlings. Mrs. Blair has a mynah bird which had never said anything until the first blast, and then it said clearly: "Leave me out of here." Ungrammatical to be sure, but the bird was excited.

I think the starlings are attracted to Mrs. McMurty's roof because her house is older and the attic is not insulated, and the roof is warm in winter from escaping heat. I think also heaven sent the starlings to Mrs. McMurty's roof to punish her for writing a letter to the newspapers one winter asking people to feed the birds — but only deserving birds. She pointedly left starlings off the approved list, and the next day the starlings were on her roof in the hundreds.

I have been feeding birds for years, starlings too, and I feed them with chicken feed and booze on very cold days and during and after blizzards and when Jack Frost comes tippy-toeing.

I want to tell you something. Birds are not frightened away when you feed them booze. What happens is, when you come down the next morning for breakfast, they are outside tapping on the windowpane with their beaks, asking for more! They dive-bomb cats. They go around looking for owls to fight. There is a great deal of latent hostility in birds, I have found, and it doesn't take much booze to release it.

I don't try to get birds drunk. But when it is cold, a little quick heat helps. I give them a very cheap bourbon, I must admit. But are they connoisseurs? And if it is good enough for *me* to drink, should I get them a better brand?

Mrs. McMurty says to feed them suet — all except starlings, which are not *deserving*. But I don't go for the usual suet routine. Why should I increase their cholesterol count?

People say: "Are you trying to make alcoholics out of birds?" And I say: "It is better to get a bird plastered than it is to give it arteriosclerosis with suet." Maybe if Mrs. McMurty fed the starlings booze too, they'd stay off her roof out of gratitude. They're too smart to spoil a good thing.

CHAPTER V

The Dibbles

One of Our Leaders in my neighborhood is Mr. Dibble whose dog used to throw sticks into the lake and this fellow would plunge in and bring them back. It started as a big gag but the dog has no sense of humor. Very soon the dog began to regard this as the natural state of affairs, the dog throwing sticks for the master to fetch back.

"Gee," Dibble told his wife, "I don't know how it got started exactly but Prince insists that it is his prerogative to throw sticks and that it is my duty to bring them back. And I think some of the neighbors are talking."

And his wife said, "Well, if it bothers you to fetch sticks back to Prince, I will go down to the lake with you and throw in sticks and you can fetch them back to *me*." And he said, "Well, gee, that's more like it!" And they were both pretty happy about it until a friend got him aside and whispered, "I don't know of any other marriage where the wife throws sticks in the lake for the husband to retrieve." And Dibble replied, "I don't either but it keeps her happy and it is a small price to pay for a happy marriage."

Well, the other day we discovered that Mrs. Dibble reads stories to him at night about the Fuzzy Rabbit. "Now it is storybook time," she says, "and we will hear more about the Fuzzy Wabbit." And he curls up with the children to listen.

The way we found out about it was that a few of us were going into a place to make the welkin ring a little, and we invited him to accompany us and maybe pick up a round or two. And he said, "I would like to go with you fellows but if I don't get home by 7 P.M. I will miss the Fuzzy Rabbit. It is a great story and my wife reads it extraordinarily well, with gestures and changing inflections, and she brings it alive...."

And we said, "Chee-e!" And he said, "For a while there she was reading Chicken Little, but frankly, I never got with Chicken Little. For my money Chicken Little is a nudnick. Nothing ever happens. But there is some real action with the Fuzzy Rabbit."

It seems one night he heard his children screaming with delight when his wife was reading to them at bedtime and he went in to listen. It was a pretty horrible story about some gorgeous girl named Rapunzel who was locked in a tower by a wicked witch. The king's son discovered she was there and gave her a holler. "How's to come up and set a spell there, Beautiful?" and she let down her long golden braids and he climbed up. She had a very healthy scalp and deeply-rooted hair, and she winced a little, but anything to have company.

He began going up regularly, and one night the witch caught him and cut Rapunzel's hair so the king's son took a nasty fall and got himself blinded. At this point Dibble complained to his wife, "I do not believe this is any kind of story to read to growing children. This girl in the tower may have been a good girl, but she was certainly over-trusting, and I believe the witch, in cutting her hair, was only trying to preserve her reputation."

And his wife said, "You can't stay and listen to these stories if you are going to be on the wrong side." But the next night she began to read about the Fuzzy Rabbit, and he was delighted because he could *identify*. He really could.

He also says his wife has an oversupply of maternal affection, and to read to him as well as to the children helps her use it up. "If she did not use it up at home," he says, "I am afraid she would be all over the neighborhood looking for someone else to mother."

We saw her at a recent party. She is a slim, sultry woman who speaks husky like Cleopatra going down the Nile, and it would be no hardship to have her read the Fuzzy Rabbit to you or to fetch back sticks she threw.

*   *   *

So we are at the Dibbles' the other night for dinner, and the kids are upstairs. And Mrs. Dibble's mother, who is pretty near eighty-five and is a strong personality in her own right, is up in her room with a bottle of brandy and is looking at risque pictures in her stereoscope.

Nothing really offensive, you understand. She insisted one night I look at her pictures while she sat by giggling, and mostly they were about fellows watching girls climb aboard streetcars and calling out, "Oh, you chicken!" And there was one I remember of a masher tipping his hat to an obviously decent girl and saying, "Ah there, Belinda!" It was freighted with the most sinister meaning but you couldn't really say it was prurient.

Well, anyway, I like to think of the Dibbles as a good typical, American family — maybe even the *sanest* family in our neighborhood.

So Mr. Dibble is carving the roast pheasant, with feathers — you are supposed to eat the feathered tails, too, I guess, but I have never been able to get them down. All of a sudden he puts down the carving knife and fork and hollers, "Fire drill! Fire drill! Fire drill!" And Mrs. Dibble says, "Oh, Clyde! Not now! Really!" And then she says to us, "It's just a family fire drill. You sit here, we'll be back in a moment." By this time he is out on the front lawn, and the kids come sliding down a knotted rope outside the dining room window, and Mr. Dibble's mother-in-law sails by the French doors toward the back yard in a faded robe I think the Salvation Army must have sent back to her.

Green Eyes and I don't know what to do. We just eat a few olives, and pretty soon the family comes in and Mrs. Dibble says, "I believe fire drills are no good when they are expected." And he explains he read somewhere it is good business to have family fire drills, and he says, "We were forced to it. Mrs. Dibble's lovely mother smokes cigars in bed." And Mrs. Dibble says, "Oh, Clyde! Really!"

And he says, "You can't tell the old lady anything. She gets up every morning with cigar ashes all over her nighty." And she said, "Clyde, I am not going to let you leave these people with the impression my mother is a *character* or something. She smokes very little, she smokes a dainty little perfumed cigarette, not more than four or five packs a day, and she only smoked in bed once." And he said, "We only caught her once."

But, you see, it is my belief that Mr. Dibble really thought up the fire drill idea to work off his own hostility. It is his one chance in that house to holler and to have everyone *jump.*

*   *   *

We had a pretty good snowstorm in our neighborhood the other day, and Mr. Dibble was delighted. You see, his wife gave him one of those baby tractors for Christmas. You can sit on it and push snow around like a bulldozer in the winter. You can also sit on it and mow lawns in the summer. And it will also till and turn over earth, and harrow, and I don't know what else, and this is very handy if you want to plant your front lawn in potatoes or alfalfa.

The reason Mrs. Dibble got the tractor for Mr. Dibble is that he has a nervous heart. It gets nervous any time he is confronted by work. She reasoned that if work could be made *fun,* why he might work a little around the yard. Also this tractor is cute. She had a rear-view mirror put on it, and a transistor radio, and an impertinent little bulb horn which goes tweet, tweet, and for a while there, Mr. Dibble was driving it around the neighborhood very gaily and even the drag-race set was so envious they flipped.

Mrs. Dibble's mother was dead against it. She told her daughter that the first thing Mr. Dibble would do when it snowed again would be plow off The Widow's sidewalk. And Mrs. Dibble said, "Oh, Mother, I wish you wouldn't be so hostile. He can't do anything right to suit you." And the old lady said, "All I have got against him is he is stupid."

So we had our snowstorm, and Mr. Dibble revved up his tractor and plowed a path from his garage down the street right to The Widow's sidewalk.

He came down the street going tweet, tweet the whole way. I know because I was one of several fellows helping shovel snow off The Widow's sidewalk by hand, and The Widow was out there with us in her ski pants being grateful and mighty picturesque. Dibble's baby tractor makes a horrible racket, but you could hear him shouting over the noise, "It's Lochinvar, come to your rescue out of the West! May I help you, My Pretty Lady?" I mean, a real showoff, the biggest mouth in town.

And The Widow wiggled over and said, "It's the best offer I've had today."

She forgot the rest of us who are in grave personal danger just in being there. All except myself. I had written permission from Green Eyes, but the other fellows had just sneaked off to The Widow's house. I cleaned off my own walk first and then asked Green Eyes if she minded if I helped clean up The Widow's, and I thought she was very open-minded about it. She said, "Why should I mind? I can look out the window every two minutes and see exactly what you're doing." She trusts me.

Mrs. Dibble began wondering how her husband was coming along with their sidewalk, and she discovered she was fresh out of husband. So she followed the tractor tracks down to The Widow's. But by this time, Mr. Dibble was

ploughing Mrs. Blair's walk next door. Mrs. Blair, with her
new hairdo, looks frightfully sexy and mysterious, and *she*,
not The Widow, was sitting behind Mr. Dibble. Mrs. Dibble
was speechless. She was prepared to deal with The Widow
but not Mrs. Blair who is her best friend — or who used to be.

Happily, Mr. Dibble shouted, "And here comes the prettiest girl of them all!" and invited his wife to get behind him.
For the rest of the day they ploughed *everyone's* sidewalk.
Mrs. Dibble told Green Eyes she felt like a silly schoolgirl
again. But she also said she thinks her husband is guilty of
something and she is going to punish him just as soon as she
figures out what it is.

*   *   *

Mr. Dibble was down at our house the other evening, and
he is having trouble with his mother-in-law. She has taken to
hammering on the waterpipes with a bath brush when not
enough hot or cold water comes out of the bathtub or shower
fixtures to please her. She lived in an apartment so many
years she can't break the habit. She can't be persuaded that
there is no janitor or superintendent downstairs to hear her
and respond to her signal.

Both Mr. and Mrs. Dibble have carefully explained to her
that theirs is a new house and that the contractor probably
skimped and put in pipes that were too small, and that's why
the plumbing grumbles behind the walls and why the faucets
are "starved." But Dibble's mother-in-law is not interested in
explanations.

When she turns on a faucet she wants a deluge and not a
drizzle. And when he goes into his small-pipe routine she
fixes him with a look of outright disbelief. It has long been
obvious to her that every time the man who married her
daughter opens his mouth, he is lying.

Mr. Dibble told me that the old lady began hammering on
the pipes the other night, and he said to his wife: "Will you for

heaven sake tell the old bag that when she hammers on the pipes there is no janitor or superintendent down here to answer her. There is only me. And no woman in the world is going to get me out of my chair to go anywhere by hammering on the pipes."

And Mrs. Dibble who is one of the most aggressive women I know said, "Your mother isn't very smart, either." And he said: "We are not talking about *my* mother. We are discussing *your* mother. My mother may have her peculiarities but she does *not* hammer on pipes! *Your* mother takes the brandy upstairs and gets loaded and smokes cigars and then hammers on the pipes."

And she said: "Oh, you are impossible!"

The hammering continued until Mr. Dibble was about to jump out of his skin, so he went upstairs and shouted through his mother-in-law's bathroom door: "What the devil is wrong now?" And the old lady said: "I am not going to talk to you because you weren't nice to me at dinner. I want the superintendent."

And he said: "Mother, there *is* no superintendent here. How many times have we told you? I am the one who has to fix things around here." And she said: "No wonder nothing happens when a person turns on the faucet." And Mr. Dibble said he got chest pains and dizziness and double-vision from frustration. You see, his mother-in-law has money, a lot of it, and he only dares discipline her up to a point.

So he said: "Mother. The dishwasher is going in the kitchen and the washing machine is going in the basement and there is just not enough water left for your bath. It's that simple."

And she said: "Oh, sure. You always *were* a smooth-talker."

Mr. Dibble came down to our house, and a couple of hours later his wife came after him. She's a witch, too, you know, the head witch around here actually, and she babied him a little and bewitched him and led him away.

When Mrs. Dibble puts Mr. Dibble under a very powerful spell, it is so strong that Mr. Thorndyke in the house immediately north feels it also. He describes the sensation as like putting your finger into a live electric light socket. He hadn't done anything, of course, and he complained to Mrs. Thorndyke that Mrs. Dibble was bewitching him. Mr. Thorndyke's wife is a witch, too. She is continually saying witch-like things such as "All right, Harry, that is your fourth drink and that will be the last!" The witches in our neighborhood stand together, and Mrs. Thorndyke refused to neutralize Mrs. Dibble's spell from next door. "You probably deserve it," she said.

I know all the neighborhood witches because they belong to the Garden Club, which meets at our house every month, and I listen at the top of the stairs to what they say. The last time they were here there was a lively discussion about a television show concerning a witch, and it was the consensus that the people producing the show know utterly nothing about witches. They said that when a wife is a real witch she would never confess it to her husband and throw away such a great advantage. I did pull two straws out of a broom up at my desk and two of the ladies did leave early with blinding headaches.

* * *

The rumor is going around the neighborhood again — just as it does every Easter — that Mrs. Dibble's mother handed out risque Easter eggs. It's not true, and I want to scotch the story.

I received one of the old lady's eggs, and I saw the one she gave The Widow, and there was nothing risque about either of them. They weren't conventional, that's true. They merely reflected, I thought, the distorted view of life of a woman who had once owned a carnival and had met more than her share of grifters and con men and geeks and strippers, and the occasional gonif.

She decorated her Easter eggs like voluptuous young ladies, and although Green Eyes didn't fully approve, she did let me have my egg beside my breakfast plate Easter morning. But she made me throw it away two weeks later.

Mrs. Dibble's mother slipped out of the house one afternoon before Easter and came down here and leaned on the doorbell, and when I opened the door she handed me this decorated egg. "Why good heavens," I said. "It has just been laid! It is still warm." And she said: "I had to bring it here down the front of my dress. My daughter frisks me pretty carefully these days whenever I leave the house."

And I said: "I think you have a great deal of talent and a nice sense of humor." And she said: "I am inviting you to a big blast at our house Easter afternoon." And I said: "Somehow it doesn't seem quite right to have a blast on Easter, do you think? And does your daughter know you are inviting people to your house for a blast?" And she said: "Some joker is always spoiling my fun. Who asked you?"

I showed the egg to Green Eyes and she flew to the telephone and called Mrs. Dibble, and almost immediately I heard Mrs. Dibble on her front porch shrieking, *"Muth-er! Muth-er!"* When she wants to, her voice will carry a good mile over a factory whistle.

* * *

Mr. Dibble had a terrible shock one night. He discovered that his wife had been unfaithful. He had no idea.

When I told Green Eyes she said: "Oh come now. Mrs. Dibble? I don't believe it."

And I said: "He was telling us on the bus this morning. He found this newspaper in his basement last night, with a sample ballot which Mrs. Dibble had marked. She voted against every single one of his candidates."

And she said: "Oh, that."

And I said: "What worse can a wife do to a husband? It is

even worse than if she had something going for herself on the other end of town. If a husband can't trust his wife to go into the voting booth and vote the way he told her, what is there left to marriage?"

And she said: "Mr. Dibble can't be positive how his wife voted, can he? He'll really *never know,* will he?"

And I said: "The evidence is conclusive. The paper had been folded. She probably carried it in her bag to the polls, and when she got behind the curtain she sneaked a look at it."

And she said: "Oh pooh. She may have changed her mind at the last moment."

And I said: "Mr. Dibble said he watched her feet below the curtains and he said her feet were moving around mighty suspicious."

And she said: "I don't like to bring this up, but has it ever occurred to you that if Mrs. Dibble did vote against her husband's candidates how badly she must have felt to know that her *own husband* was going to cancel *her* vote with his?"

And I said: "You got it all wrong. Boy, are *you* mixed up. It is the husband's job to decide how the family will vote. Women don't vote on broad general principles. They get all tied up with emotions. Like Grandma, for instance. She will vote against a guy because she thinks his eyes are too close together."

Mr. Dibble has one consolation. He *knows* his mother-in-law went right down the line with him. She stood in the booth and hollered out the name of everyone she voted for. She's very hearty.

CHAPTER VI

The Animals

Caesar, the great big old friendly St. Bernard up the street, is staying with us for three weeks while his folks, the Peabodys, are in Hawaii. I have to be very quiet around the house now because Caesar sleeps in until noon. He is in our guest room, in a four-posted Colonial bed. He sleeps in a double bed at Peabodys', too, also in their guest room, and sometimes when they have a guest and forget to notify Caesar that he is to sleep somewhere else, why he gets into bed with the guest.

There is no problem about taking care of Caesar. Of course he drools a little but his party manners are inexorably correct. He takes breakfast by himself, and lunch, but he eats with us at dinner. The Peabodys wanted to provide us with three weeks' food for him but I said we could handle that easily enough. The only place I would need help would be in providing Caesar with enough gin for three weeks to peddle around the neighborhood. You see he wears this keg which the Peabodys (and now we) keep full of martinis. And he goes up to the bus stop and all around the neighborhood looking for lost and fainting travelers and gives them martinis. He also carries paper cups and a small bottle of pickled onions. I suppose he should carry brandy for lost and fainting travelers but we have found — or the Peabodys have — that lost and fainting travelers in this particular neighborhood much prefer to be revived with martinis, very dry.

Peabody is furnishing the gin. He dropped off an even dozen bottles the night before Caesar arrived here, and I keep filling up the keg with martinis and Caesar goes out and comes back in an hour or two with the keg empty. A great many people around here are getting lost, obviously.

Caesar came down here by himself when the Peabodys left. He carried a tote-bag in his mouth with his toilet articles — his toothbrush and paste, combs and brushes, and a few pills the veterinarian had prescribed for his digestion. I have tried one or two of these pills myself and I believe they have done me immeasurable good. I find they do somewhat alter my attitude toward cats — I have an impulse to chase cats — but I do come to meals ravenously hungry.

I don't think the Peabodys ever go to bed until 1 A.M. at the earliest, and Caesar can't quite make out Green Eyes and me when we go to bed at 10:30. It disturbs him, as a matter of fact, and when he sees us getting undressed he looks at the clock and then at us and whines. I leave the television on for him and a late snack on the kitchen table, and anywhere between 1 A.M. and 2 A.M. we hear him getting into bed in the room across the hall. We turn the blankets and upper sheet for him, and when he is in bed he pulls them back over him. The Peabodys taught him to do that long ago.

Only once since he came to us has Caesar got loaded on his own booze. The Peabody children found that Caesar during his master's parties would sometimes go upstairs and close the drain in the bathtub and bounce the keg against the tub bottom until the cork came out and the martinis were liberated. Then he would lick the martinis up. If a dog is going to drink, it is my feeling that he should not have to compound it with sneaky tactics like this (and then feel guilty), and I quite frankly offer him a drink at bedtime if he wants it. But I won't let him take the keg to bed. If he wants another drink, he can ask me for one.

McMurty summed it up nicely one day, I think, when we

all piled out at the bus stop and Caesar came romping up with his keg, and McMurty said: "Look, here comes Man's Best Friend — and a big dog is carrying it, too."

In addition to patrolling the neighborhood, Caesar is in business for himself over at the golf course picking up lost balls. He doesn't actually find them himself. He has a deal with a pointer who does it for him. The pointer finds and points the balls, and Caesar leisurely picks them up and brings them home in a child's sandpail, by the pailful. Peabody, Caesar's master, turns them into cash and credits Caesar with them in a savings account in the village bank. When Peabody opened the account for his dog, the bank wanted to call the papers in — banks will do *anything* for publicity these days — but Caesar refused to let anyone take his picture. He has great dignity and a sense of fitness, and he won't look at dog pictures on TV and he won't respond when you say, "Here doggie, doggie, doggie." You just better address him by his right name or you miss out on the martinis.

Caesar pays off the pointer in peanuts, dog biscuits actually, one per ball. Fuller owns the pointer and Fuller complains to Peabody whenever we all get together that Caesar is exploiting his pointer. The pointer's name is Wetter, which carries over from his puppyhood.

*   *   *

The Widow's French poodle, Fifi, a charming dog who walks around the neighborhood with every bit as much excitement in her stride as her mistress, has been hanging around our house ever since Caesar came to visit. She had paid no attention to us before, and in the past when I would say, "Here, Fifi, here, Fifi," she would give me the coldest of receptions.

But the day after Caesar arrived, she came over to breakfast and had to be restrained from going upstairs and waking up our guest. We tried to explain to her that Caesar always sacks in until noon but she wasn't believing it.

The Widow is quite disturbed by Fifi's apparent infatuation with Caesar. Fifi, she says, is looking for a husband, and The Widow doesn't think Caesar is right for her. I am not much worried that a serious romance will develop here. Caesar pays little attention to Fifi although she carries on around him with the most shameless kind of flirting. She stayed to dinner the other night and insisted on eating out of Caesar's dish which he accepted with amusement and a good-natured shrug. I think he is much too worldly to be taken in by such feminine tricks.

I am worried a little bit about the Dibbles' big boxer, Digger. He hasn't been around to our flower beds lately, and I asked Dibble where he was, and Dibble said they had him at the veterinarian's for treatment for a psychosis. They think he is a little nuts. Well actually, I have thought so for a long time. Digger is the only dog I ever heard of who carries a security blanket around with him, like a child.

When he was a puppy he used to worry the blanket out of his basket and take it outdoors and chew on it, and the Dibbles trained him to carry it around when he was with them — and to drag it into the car when they went for a family-type Sunday ride. Now he takes it everywhere and he is a six-year-old dog. The other dogs down at the corner hydrant are puzzled, I think, when he shows up dragging his blanket, and they react to the blanket exactly as they do to the hydrant.

Mrs. Dibble picks the blanket up every morning with a long stick and throws it in her washer-dryer, and Digger won't go out until it has been restored to him. It was a cute gag when he was a puppy, but now it has become a fixation.

Dr. Wynn, the vet, has never psychoanalyzed a dog before but he is very anxious to try, and he is not going to charge the Dibbles except for Digger's food. I don't know much about Dr. Wynn except that I have heard that whenever his wife wonders if he is sick, why she feels his nose.

I remember at the Fullers' last week, Dr. Wynn was moping, off in a corner alone, and Mrs. Wynn went up to him and said: "Do you feel all right?" And he said: "I just feel kind of tired." And she felt his nose and said: "You're all right. Your nose is cold and moist."

Well, Dr. Wynn said at the Fullers' party that Fifi, The Widow's big French poodle, could expect her babies about June 8. She is already at the halfway mark and carrying her litter very well. The Widow is feeding her cod liver oil and raw eggs and all the meat she wants, and when Fifi is visiting at the Peabodys', her husband's home, she eats better than the family does.

The way they do it, Fifi and her husband, Caesar, the Peabodys' big, friendly, martini-serving St. Bernard, stay at The Widow's one week and at the Peabodys' the next week. Caesar is resigned to her attentions, and Fifi believes that a husband ought to be with a wife constantly at such a time as this.

The Widow still is sore at me because Caesar and Fifi got married when Caesar was a guest in my home. I didn't attend the marriage and I didn't even know it had taken place but it didn't surprise me any. Fifi tried by every ruse imaginable to get into our house when Caesar was there, and I never saw such a disgraceful display of sex appeal.

Caesar looks sadder than ever and I think it was a shock to him to realize that he still has the baser instincts of a dog when all this time he was thinking of himself as people.

If Dr. Wynn is able to separate Digger from his security blanket, I hope he next psychoanalyzes Wetter, the Fullers' pointer. Wetter's name dates back to puppyhood when he showed an unusual preoccupation with carpets and he still does. He is a fine hunting dog but when he is not hunting birds he is hunting carpets, and whereas the bird season is rather short, the carpet season is all year long and his achievements are astonishing.

Joe Oedipus, the psychiatrist's cat, is becoming a fat alcoholic but Dr. Spook, his master, doesn't seem to worry much about it. You see, Joe Oedipus is very fond of canapes and hors d'oeuvres, and you never give a cocktail party but what he comes up to the front door and walks in with a guest. Then he takes his place at the bar with the menfolk, while his mother, who follows him everywhere, crawls under the sofa and watches him.

Everyone gives Joe canapes that are spread with liver and they frequently pour him drinks. Not very strong, to be sure, but lately he has been asking for more and more. He carries his booze well but the food is beginning to show. Dr. Spook says Joe Oedipus probably does not drink more than he should. He says cats are much smarter than people — they will only eat and drink what they need. I disagree. I think Joe Oedipus is eating and drinking to escape his mother.

* * *

There was a big auction party at The Widow's to find homes for the puppies of Wetter and Fifi, half pointer and half French poodle. Judging from their behavior as puppies they are more like their daddy, Wetter, than like their mama, Fifi, and she didn't do a very good job of training them, either.

As a matter of fact Fifi has been an appallingly casual mother. She wasn't about to nurse them at first and The Widow was desperate until I suggested that Fifi be locked up with her pups in The Widow's backyard sauna until she darn well decided to nurse them. It worked. After a day of barking and whining that she was not going to give up the best years of her life to nursing six pups, she finally became resigned to it because there was nothing else in the sauna for her to do. She still growls and racks out her teeth pretty good when she sees me.

Fifi has been shameless from the start. First, when she got pregnant, she tried to make it appear that my old friend Caesar, the big St. Bernard up the street, was the daddy, and the Peabodys made a deal with The Widow under which the two dogs alternated living in the two houses every week.

Caesar wore a continual look of disbelief and puzzlement during this period because, I guess, he couldn't remember any honeymoon. I suspect Caesar figured he was loaded the night of the marriage.

It wasn't until the pups arrived and the veterinarian told The Widow that Wetter, not Caesar, was surely the father that Caesar regained his usual genial aplomb — and Fifi was exposed for the low character she really is. No other lady dog in the neighborhood would have anything to do with Wetter, and none of the humans, either. Some pointer he is! He doesn't know north from up. He will be pointing toward a bird and you will say to him, "Wetter, are you *sure* that's where it is?" and he will immediately change his point to some other direction.

Dr. Spook says Wetter is very unsure of himself and that his misbehavior is an indication that he is sore at human society. Dr. Spook says, "His preoccupation with living room carpets in people's houses shows that he is more critic than he is dog."

Well, when Wetter's and Fifi's puppies showed every sign of carrying on their father's tradition, nobody wanted them. The Widow finally decided to offer them as door prizes for charity, for the PTA missions overseas, and she had this party where if you won a pup you had to take it home *that very night!* All except the top winner. If you were the top winner, you didn't have to take a pup. And I was the top winner.

I am afraid that some of the people who took pups home that night didn't realize their heritage until a day or two later. Of course, their children were delighted and took care of them next morning after a fashion until their parents were up again, but I notice that the rug-cleaning truck had been outside all six houses lately.

With a mother like Fifi and a father like Wetter I am afraid not much can be expected of these little doggies. But maybe with loving care and a good example and a lot of intensive study of the points of the compass, they may turn out to be some kind of pointer. Right now you can't tell. There is a lot of the natural-born stool pigeon in Fifi, and her three girl puppies have inherited it. Fuller got one of the females and he tells me she is already pointing at him accusingly every time he opens a can of beer.

*   *   *

People *try,* sometimes against very heavy odds, to love and understand and get along with their neighbors. Even if they live in a neighborhood like mine.

Mrs. Peterson lives in a nice house, but she still keeps chickens and lately the rooster has been getting up pretty early and getting the rest of us up with him. This rooster, who has the unloveliest personality I ever encountered in a rooster, will even get up and crow when somebody comes down the alley late at night and the headlights sweep his pen.

We are not bothered so much by Mrs. Peterson's rooster when Dr. Spook is home. Dr. Spook lives across the alley from Mrs. Peterson, and every evening he drops something in the rooster's yard which sedates it pretty good.

Well, when Dr. Spook is home and sedating Mrs. Peterson's rooster (without her knowledge, of course), the rooster gets up about noon, and even then he scarcely ever crows. He staggers around and croaks a little, and the hens come up to. the wire separating them and say: "Well, hello, there! And how are you this fine day?" And the rooster says: "Ga-rad-a-here. Leave me alone." (I may be the only writer in the world who brings you authentic chicken talk.)

I believe Mrs. Peterson's rooster is in great danger. I believe the Carters' oldest girl may try to kill him. The Carter girl's boy friend brought her home at 3 A.M. last Sunday, and the headlights woke up Mrs. Peterson's rooster and he got up and crowed and awakened the people in the houses all around. Mr. Carter stuck his head out the window and demanded to know why his daughter was being brought home at such an hour, and the Carter girl was dreadfully embarrassed. She talked right back at her father and told him it was none of his business (which it certainly *was*), and then she cried, and the boy tried to explain, and he is really a good kid, and now the neighborhood is divided. All the wives and mothers are on Mr. Carter's side, and all we husbands and fathers are on the kid's side (unless we have daughters).

If Mrs. Peterson's rooster, whose time clock was mixed up badly anyway, even before Dr. Spook began to sedate him — if the rooster hadn't hollered copper, the Carter girl could have slipped quietly into her home and it would have been a simply wonderful evening. Now it is a Big Thing and her father is a tyrant and her mother is dumb, and her world is in ashes. The nicest boy she ever met will never, never go out with her again, and she is going to kill herself.

It is against all the zoning ordinances for Mrs. Peterson to keep chickens, and it doesn't help any of our property values, either, for Mrs. Peterson to plant most of her front lawn in potatoes. Mrs. Peterson is a difficult woman, and it is hard to love her, but she has her troubles, too. The President of the United States reads all her mail and listens to all the telephone conversations she has with her sister, Agnes, in South Dakota. Agnes and Mrs. Peterson can hear the clicks on the telephone when the White House cuts in, and Mrs. Peterson frequently shouts: "Get off the line, there, Mr. President." It all started when the President didn't reappoint Agnes to her postmistress job. The President moved the post office right out of Agnes' store down the road a full ten miles to a new building.

Mrs. Peterson is not aware that her rooster acts funny when Dr. Spook is home. She doesn't realize yet that her rooster only goes "cockle." There hasn't been a "doodle-doo" out of him for months, except the last two weeks when Dr. Spook has been away.

Nobody wants a big rhubarb at the county zoning commission about Mrs. Peterson's chickens, and there is some question, anyway, whether you can stop a person from having chickens if they don't sell the eggs or the chickens commercially. Mrs. Peterson says her chickens are pets, and she goes out and talks to them, and they talk back to her, and maybe they *are* pets, I don't know.

The community club sent a committee around to talk to Mrs. Peterson about the chickens, but she very quickly discovered that the President had sent them, and she ordered the committee right out of her house. But when she comes to my house to Garden Club meetings, she is one of the nicest ladies I know. And stable.

*   *   *

There is a small barn owl who lives from time to time in my upstairs porch, right outside my bedroom. He flies in during the early morning and stays in the warmth of the porch during the day, and then flies out when we open the windows at bedtime. During the day he perches sleepily on an old chair we put out for his use, and his house manners are not completely beyond reproach, but he tries hard to be neat.

I have tried to feed suet to this owl and he won't touch it. What he would like me to feed him is a mouse, but I really don't have the time to go out and catch mice for him. I feel I have discharged my obligation as a reasonably decent human being if I offer him a warm bed during the day and an occasional breakfast of chopped meat.

This owl flies away for a month or two but keeps coming back. We have a very nice relationship, and we talk to each other. I get up in the morning and I see him on the back of the chair, and I say to him: "Good morning there, owl. I guess a certain bird I know has been helling around all night, hey?" And then he says: "Whoo?" and I say: "Let's not be evasive about this. It should be very easy for you to guess." And he says "Whoo?" Great dialogue, but then he is not as smart as owls are supposed to be. I suspect that none of them are. I sometimes say jovially to this owl: "Are you a wise old owl?" and he says "Whoo?" again like a stuck phonograph record. I don't think there is an idea in his head. But we don't know what *he* thinks about *me*, either, do we?

*   *   *

I was talking to this fellow who had just come in from Jasper National Park in Alberta. He said he had played golf with a bear. He said he and two other fellows started out from the Lodge one morning and the bear joined them on the third hole, making it a foursome.

The fellow said: "We asked him if he minded our playing through but he wanted to join us. He played right along. Had his own clubs but no cart. His long game was terrific. I mean he was driving them 600 yards. What shoulders! But his short game was only fair. Even so, he birdied two holes."

And I said: "What I can't understand is how can bears *afford* to play at Jasper. I've heard it is one of the most expensive places in Canada." And he said: "The Lodge has tried from time to time to collect from the bears, but the bears never have any money. It's because they don't have pockets, I suppose. If bears had pockets and could carry money, I have no doubt they would pay willingly for the privilege of playing at Jasper. The bears we met were a rather decent sort."

And I said: "This bear that played around with you fellows, was it a girl bear or a boy bear?"

And he said: "Good heavens! It never occurred to me to wonder. But from the length of his drives I would say he was a boy bear, definitely. He never once drove off from the women's tee."

And I said: "Did you ever meet him again?"

And he said: "No, I was at the Lodge for the one day, but we did invite him along to our cottage for a snack in the afternoon. He sat on the porch and licked off our dishes."

And I said: "You *could* have invited him in."

And he said: "The Lodge frowns on that. But I don't want you to conclude that the bears are in any way excluded at Jasper. In the big early September tournament there is always a division for bears."

CHAPTER VII

The Doctors

Our own neighborhood psychiatrist, Dr. Spook, doesn't practice here, of course. He practices downtown. Nobody in our neighborhood wants to be adjusted although a good many of us could use it.

Spook is a terrible name for a psychiatrist, and I haven't often mentioned his name before because he becomes resentful and anxious every time he hears it pronounced or sees it in print. He went to court once to have it changed but he came up before a judge who could see no valid reason whatever for such a change. The judge was a Spook, too, and he lectured Dr. Spook on the illustrious history of the Spook line — right back to old Charlemagne Spook, II, the greatest knight of them all, who rode to his wedding in a full suit of armor in a driving rain and rusted tight in his saddle. They had to carry him into the church in a sitting position to the altar, and the reception was postponed twelve hours until the village blacksmith could pry him free.

Dr. Spook listened to this account without much relish because the Spooks from whom he descended are only two generations old. The family was originally Spoech (pronounced "Speck") from Middle Europe. Dr. Spook's grandfather had the name changed ten years after he arrived in America because he tired of the nickname everyone gave him here. "Fly," they called him. "Fly" Spoeck.

It is a funny thing about names. As a psychiatrist, and a very good one, too, the name "Spook" is a disadvantage and an embarrassment to Dr. Spook. But if he had chosen to operate a trick and puzzle store, his name would have been his fortune.

What I was going to tell you is that everywhere Dr. Spook goes socially, people come up and tell him their dreams. The other night at the Blairs', Mrs. McMurty told him about *her* dream. "The whole top of the Episcopal church, steeple and all, detached itself from the building and chased me down the street." And Dr. Spook said: "Chee!" and "Sheesh!"

And she said: "Do you think my dream had any significance?" And he said: "Not when I am out socially, I don't." And she said: "I was wondering whether I should talk to somebody about it." And Dr. Spook said: "By all means. I think you should talk to the rector of the Episcopal Church. If his church tower is chasing women around here in their dreams, I think he should know."

A lot of people come up to Dr. Spook at social affairs and pose a problem about "a friend." "I have a friend," they say, "who is always thinking of ways to kill her husband, and I wonder if it is dangerous." And Dr. Spook says: "I doubt very much you have such a friend. I think you are talking about yourself and your own death wishes for your own husband. And my advice to you is — go ahead. But keep it tidy." And then they say: "I resent what you said because I love my husband and the last thing in this world I would do is kill him." And Dr. Spook says, "Oh, sure."

I heard The Widow come up to him one night and say: "I have this funny recurrent dream where I am chasing every man in the neighborhood," and Dr. Spook said: "I don't believe it is a dream at all. I think it is a conscious fantasy. I think you *are* chasing every man in the neighborhood." And The Widow walked away highly displeased.

The women around here all distrust Dr. Spook, and they are afraid he can read their minds. But they do envy his wife, Mrs. Spook. The doctor runs a completely permissive household, no one has compulsions, and Mrs. Spook often lies in bed until noon.

* * *

Internists and surgeons everywhere look with suspicion on psychiatrists as Johnnies-Come-Lately.

I am thinking particularly about Doc Excerebro, the brain surgeon, who lives up in the next block. We all call him "Old Shaky." He is a familiar sight to all of us, the first to arrive at a cocktail party and the last to leave, but always up at dawn, shaking all over, off to the surgery.

There are many famous stories about his exploits. I guess he is one of the best in the business. They say he was on a hunting trip once and had to perform a frontal lobotomy on himself using local anaesthesia, a hand mirror, and a few instruments he brought along in his emergency bag. The operation was entirely successful, he took a short nap after it, and had a good dinner ready for the whole gang when they came in to camp that evening.

I find it somewhat difficult to believe this story because a lobotomy involves removing part of the skull with a trepanning tool and I should think it would be an awkward procedure without help. Everyone on that camping trip, however, swears the story is true. Dr. Excerebro, however, modestly says it wasn't really a frontal lobotomy he performed unaided on himself. What he actually did, he says, was take out his own gall bladder.

"I had nothing much else to do," he says. "I am not much of a reader, and all we had in camp were girlie magazines, anyway. It was my turn to stay in camp all day, and it seemed as good a time as any to get rid of a gall bladder which had been causing me a good deal of trouble."

The story had wide circulation around town and finally got into one of the newspapers. The article mentioned Dr. Excerebro by name and carried his picture (together with an artist's sketch of him taking out his own gall bladder). This publicity infuriated the medical society and they had him up before a committee and they said he had put medicine back a thousand years. They said it was all right for him to be a big exhibitionist and operate on himself *provided* he kept it out of the newspapers, and they particularly resented the operating gown he wore in the picture which had his name on it and also the legend in big letters: "Brain Surgery."

Happily, the censure never went beyond a mild official rebuke because Dr. Excerebro is quite generous with doctors who refer cases to him, and he is loved by the whole medical fraternity — except the gall bladder specialists who felt that if he was going to have his gall bladder out he should have called in one of them instead. They said it would have been easy enough for him to have included a gall bladder man among his hunting companions.

Well, what I was going to tell you was about the big hassle he got into with Dr. Spook, our psychiatrist, who is a pretty competent all-around doctor himself except that he has this psychosis about chickens. He is afraid of them and admits it freely.

We were all at the Coopers' and Dr. Excerebro stopped at the tenth highball because he had to operate in the morning, and he was being very rude to Dr. Spook, asking him whether he wore feathered anklets and a mask and shook gourds when he psychoanalyzed his patients. And Dr. Spook finally said that Dr. Excerebro's continual shaking suggested to him that Dr. Excerebro had missed his calling and might have gone a long way as a jazz drummer. Dr. Spook also said that the shaking meant to him that Dr. Excerebro felt very guilty about something, and went on to say that this guilt might be based on some of the fees Dr. Excerebro charges for some of his operations.

It was altogether a nasty encounter, but Dr. Excerebro brought it on and I think Dr. Spook was well within his right to defend himself and strike where it would do the most good.

Happily, another professional was present at this party — a dentist. He thought it was time that he brought this disgraceful confrontation to a stop, and he said that modern drugs would very soon put both Dr. Excerebro and Dr. Spook out of business. He said it was his understanding that new drugs and medical procedures were making both brain surgery and psychoanalysis quite unnecessary in many cases.

They both turned savagely on him, not because he was right or wrong, I think, but because he was a dentist and obviously of a lower order.

*   *   *

A new survey has just been completed by my old friend Prof. Preston Carstairs, the psychologist, to determine why women almost always go to the powder room in pairs. I mean, of course, in public places.

Like, for instance, you take your wife and another man and his wife to dinner, and if either lady wishes to repair her makeup, she will invariably invite the other lady to accompany her as though it were some Big Thing. Furthermore, when they leave the table they seem to share some secret; they become sisters of intrigue.

The professor has noticed, as I have noticed, that when one lady asks another lady if she would like to go to the powder room, the second lady scarcely ever says "No." If the second lady does say "No," the first lady probably won't go. Ladies almost never go to the powder room singly. On the other hand, men *never* ask one another to accompany them to the powder room. This is the principal difference between the behavior of the sexes in America today — maybe the *only* difference — the professor believes.

"Going to the powder room in pairs, or more, has become among American women as much a ceremonial as the changing of the guard in London," the professor said.

Like I keep telling you, Professor Carstairs is a behaviorist-psychologist, which is the worst kind. He also doubles on weekdays at the Mother Earth Canteen at reading tea leaves. Years ago he was one of the country's outstanding phrenologists, but today women want a hair stylist not a phrenologist. The professor says ruefully, "I have learned to adjust. Tea leaves really don't tell you as much about the personality and the future as head configurations do. But with a little application you can still do a passable job with orange pekoe."

Lerner, in his pamphlet "Why Women Go To The Powder Room in Multiples — or The Herd Instinct in a Curious Manifestation," advanced the theory that women went in pairs, or more, to hold pay-doors open for one another, thus saving a dime, in some instances a quarter. But Wernick thoroughly discredited this interesting speculation. Wernick said his wife told *him* that women don't need friends to hold the doors open for one another; even utter strangers will do this for one another instinctively. She said that women the world over regard the pay-powder-room as a masculine intrusion into a purely feminine world. I'll never forget, speaking from my own experience, when Green Eyes, my wife, once encountered a half-dollar powder room, and was furious, and came back to the table with another woman and said explosively: "Who does *he* think *he* is!" It was her unshakable assumption that some crass commercial *man* was responsible.

Professor Carstairs concludes that women travel in pairs to the powder room out of a sense of needing "safety" and chaperonage. It would look funny, they say, for their husbands to accompany them to the door and wait outside to accompany them back to the table. Also, it gives two women an opportunity to discuss *other* women at the same table. I believe that women understand this, and that is why sometimes *every* woman at a large table will rise and go to the powder room at the same time as a precaution against being talked about.

I am sorry the professor was not permited to pursue his research to the ultimate. He had planned to bug a few powder rooms to eavesdrop on what was being said there. Unhappily, Mrs. Carstairs caught up with him one night in a deadfall after having searched the town for hours. Mrs. Carstairs ended the project then and there.

Dr. Carstairs is engaged at the moment on a top-secret project. And for once his wife approves because it does not involve research with the other sex.

What the professor is working on now is the development of a strain of bacteria which will consume old automobile bodies and turn them into common garden fertilizer. And after that he confidently hopes to develop another strain of bacteria which will consume the concrete in freeways and convert them into natural, fertile ground, on which vegetables can again flourish. He is looking now for a first-class bacteriologist, who is also a good gin-rummy player, to become his associate, and he hopes to come up with something before the year is out.

Professor Carstairs boldly faces the seriousness of the old cars and concrete problem, and his choice of a federal agency to solve it is the Department of Agriculture. "We need a bug," he says, "that will attack rusted metal, and if it attacks new cars as well, I'm not going to worry. And then with automobiles out of the way, we can proceed to do something about freeways. Scatter a few vials of bacteria-containing solution on a freeway on your way home some night, and within a month it will be a field again, rich in iron."

I suppose there will be scoffers but I am confident the professor will prevail. Like I have told you before, he was forced into psychology from some of the more exact sciences because of his unconventionality and the refusal of his teachers to recognize his genius. He was soaring like a rocket in meteorology until the day he discovered two snowflakes exactly *alike*. He was drummed out of meteorology because his two identical snowflakes contradicted everything meteorology had held sacred about snowflakes.

Something similar happened to him in physiology. He discovered two fingerprints which were absolutely identical. Even the FBI was confounded. And here again he was dismissed because if word ever got out that the fingerprints of some people exactly matched the fingerprints of others, why our whole economy could come tumbling down. The FBI tailed him for years.

Well, we'll see what comes of the junk-car-eating bugs.

CHAPTER VIII

The Bazettis

I am afraid the Bazettis are not much help in our neighborhood. They are wonderful people personally, you understand, so gay and friendly and hospitable. If you go over there
to complain that one of their kids has pinched your paper,
why they sit you down to a bottle of their homemade wine
and insist you drink it to the dregs. They sing and drink toasts
and make extravagant gestures.

They've never been to the Old Country (indeed, Mrs.
Bazetti is an Irish girl) but they talk about Rome and Florence
and Venice as though they were only up the road a piece, and
they are continually running out of the house with some
Italian gourmet delicacy for you to taste. Only last Thursday
Mr. Bazetti came out of his house with his napkin tucked
under his chin, carrying a platter and shouting: "You should
taste my wife's cannelloni!" Well, it was really a fusion of two
cultures, and I am still reserving my opinion. It was cannelloni stuffed with a ground-up Irish stew, and when Mrs.
Bazetti makes Irish stew she uses lots of black olives and
pimentos and tomatoes in deference to her husband's
Italian-conditioned tastes. This cannelloni was liberally
sprinkled with grated Romano cheese and finished off under
the broiler, and it *was* delicious but you couldn't really call it
cannelloni, and you couldn't call it Irish stew. If you tried to

describe it to the maitre d' in a good restaurant, he would fall over dead.

The Bazettis are the nicest people you can imagine, but now they have an old bathtub in their back yard, and our property values are dropping something awful. The bathtub in the back yard doesn't bother the neighbors across the

street, it bothers the people in six houses behind. Their patios look down into the Bazetti yard, and the bathtub, an old-timer, white with ball-and-claw feet, is the most prominent thing they see.

It is even more than a bathtub. There is a pipe and shower head attached to it, too. Mr. Bazetti was driving by a motel that was being dismantled on orders of the Board of Health, and he saw the bathtub being offered for two dollars. He told Mrs. Bazetti he was going to convert it into a "planter" or perhaps even a hotbed. And she said: "That's nice." I don't think it ever occurs to her when she looks around that some of her neighbors have spent thousands keeping their places up.

It is very difficult to disguise an old bathtub. It has a classic, easily-recognized form no matter what you do to it. Mr. Bazetti said at first he would have greenery cascading over the sides: "It will be a real beauty spot," he told Fuller. And Fuller said: "I'll bet." But the tub has been there six months now and nothing has happened yet. Mostly the Bazetti kids play in it. To them it's a boat. To the rest of us I guess you might call it a nuisance. But, even at that, it is not as disturbing as the old washing machine they took apart and never did reassemble.

The Bazettis are wonderful people, but the inside of their garage is pretty much of a mess. They have so much stuff in their garage now that they park both cars at the curb, but for some reason they never close their garage doors and the garage is in the front of the house, right across the street from the view windows of the Hillsboros' dining room.

The Hillsboros sit in their dining room and look out at the open Bazetti garage, and I want to list for you some of the things they see: a power lawn mower, a fertilizer-spreader, a wheelbarrow, a sack of peat moss, a chopping-block and axe, half a cord of fireplace wood, Mrs. Bazetti's mother's old brass bed and mattress, a white bureau with all the knobs off the drawers, lawn furniture, a baby's crib and cartons full of old clothes and bottles and newspapers which Mrs. Bazetti intends fully to give one day to the Salvation Army if she can ever remember to call. She is a very busy woman. When she makes spaghetti sauce, it takes two days.

And a toidy chair, the piece de resistance. Right in the center of the garage, separated from the rest of the mess, in a place of honor, is a toidy chair readily recognizable from a great distance. The last kid who used the Bazetti toidy chair was Angelo, and I don't suppose there will be another kid along now, but Mrs. Bazetti keeps her fingers crossed. "I just have a feeling," she tells Mr. Bazetti, "that if we ever give away the crib and the toidy chair, there will be another little stranger in the family." And Mr. Bazetti says: "By all means, keep them." No, actually what he said was: "Chee, I hope not!"

So when the Hillsboros sit down in their formal dining room in their $60,000 house and look through their view windows across the street they see the toidy chair.

Well, Mrs. Hillsboro planned to have the Daughters of the American Revolution in to lunch. Not the whole D.A.R., just the executive committee. She said to Mr. Hillsboro: "I just wish we could persuade the Bazettis to put down their garage door while the girls are here." And Mr. Hillsboro said: "What girls?" And she said: "The girls of the D.A.R. executive committee." And Mr. Hillsboro said: "Aren't you using the term 'girls' pretty loosely?" And Mrs. Hillsboro said: "Oh, now don't be nasty. I want you to ask the Bazettis to close their doors. I don't want the D.A.R. to be looking at that toidy chair all during my nice luncheon."

So Mr. Hillsboro walked across the street after dinner. He knew it was going to be a delicate business. The Bazettis are not only emotional people, quick to resent any real or fancied slight, but they are also Democrats, the only avowed Democrats in the neighborhood. Oh, I mean there are plenty of other Democrats, I suppose, but they keep it a secret. They will say: "Well, I am going in town to see a show," when actually they are going to attend a Democratic rally. But the Bazettis come right out and admit they are Democrats, and I think they take solid comfort in the thought that when the Democrats rise and come marching down our street they will be the only ones who will not be murdered in their beds.

When Bazetti answered the doorbell, Mr. Hillsboro said: "Say, Bazetti, this is sort of embarrassing to say, and I don't want you to think I am trying to live your life for you, but Mrs. Hillsboro is having a party tomorrow afternoon — a rather fancy party — and she wonders if you could pull your garage doors down."

And Bazetti said: "What's wrong with the garage doors?" And Hillsboro said: "Well, you see we have a view from our dining room into your garage, and there is a toidy chair there, and Mrs. Hillsboro — well, she just thinks it will take a little class away from her party."

And Bazetti said: "Sure, I'll pull them down. What kind of a party is it, anyway?" And Mr. Hillsboro said: "The D.A.R." and Bazetti stiffened and said: "They stay up! It wouldn't hurt the D.A.R. to look at a toidy seat." And he shut the door in Mr. Hillsboro's face. I just cite this instance to prove to you what a bunch of troublemakers the D.A.R. are in a neighborhood. They hadn't even showed up for Mrs. Hillsboro's luncheon and already they had the neighborhood split right down the middle.

* * *

People have asked me if they could buy Mrs. Stauffer's cast-iron Italian-boy hitching post, but it is already otherwise disposed of. A Norwegian family, the Swensens, bought it and they have painted it up to look like a Swede.

You see, when Mrs. Stauffer brought it home from an auction it was a colored boy. Mr. Stauffer told her it was a racial affront and that she couldn't keep it. Then Mrs. Fumbles came over and in one afternoon painted it to look like an Italian, and Mr. Stauffer approved and Mrs. Stauffer was delighted because she had maybe the only cast-iron Italian-boy hitching post anywhere in the world.

But the Bazettis next door got sore. The next thing we knew, Mrs. Bazetti did *not* invite Mrs. Stauffer to the Voters' League at her house. Poor Mrs. Stauffer was out in her yard in her gardening clothes when the dressed-up ladies began arriving at the Bazettis. They asked her if she weren't coming, and she said she didn't even know that Mrs. Bazetti was having the League that day. Mrs. Bazetti appeared at the front door to let some ladies in, and Mrs. Stauffer called to her: "I didn't know you were having the League today. I guess my notice must have miscarried." And Mrs. Bazetti said coldly: "I didn't send you one," and closed the door, and Mrs. Stauffer felt awful.

This was unusual behavior for Mrs. Bazetti. She is generally so gay and charming. The whole Bazetti family are a credit to the neighborhood, in fact. Every day is a feast day at the Bazettis. I mean you go over and ask for the loan of a nail-puller, they invite you right in to wine, a little antipasto, a couple plates of pasta with a sauce that Mrs. Bazetti only makes in the dark of the moon, and I don't know what else.

When Mr. Stauffer came home and found Mrs. Stauffer in tears because Mrs. Bazetti had snubbed her, he went right over to the Bazettis and asked them why. And Mr. Bazetti said it was because of the cast-iron hitching post which held all Italians, everywhere, up to ridicule and humiliation. And Mr. Stauffer said: "Leave us pull it up right now!" and Mr. Bazetti brightened and opened a bottle of wine, and they didn't get around to pulling the cast-iron hitching post up until two o'clock the next morning. And Mr. Bazetti said: "I have changed my mind. I rather like it now. It *does* look like me." And next day Mrs. Bazetti went over to Mrs. Stauffer's house and they put their arms around each other and cried about an hour.

The neighbors heard about this incident and the first to call me were the Swensens, our Norwegian neighbors, and they asked me to intercede with the Stauffers. They said they wanted the cast-iron hitching post, and they would paint out the Italian.

Well, it went up on their lawn about a week later, and some Swedes in the neighborhood tell me it looks like a Swede and that Swensen is going to get himself a punch in the mouth one of these days. I don't know what makes it look like a Swede. I can't tell a Swede from a Norwegian myself, but whenever I say this to a Norwegian or a Swede, either one does a quick burn. Apparently *they* can tell. So Mrs. Stauffer's innocent purchase at an auction is still stirring up neighborhood prejudices, and I am thinking of taking up a collection to buy the Swensens a cast-iron duck and four ducklings in return for the Swede hitching post. Then I will have Mrs. Fumbles come over and paint it like an Anglo-Saxon and put it up on my own parking strip. Nobody objects to a cast-iron Anglo-Saxon.

But that wasn't the end of racial trouble. Bazetti has been doing a burn ever since the Fuller party when someone touched on a very sore point again. Someone said Alonzo Sanchez de Huelva, a Spaniard, had not only discovered America, near Santo Domingo, before Columbus did, but returned home and gave Columbus a map with the American landfall in correct latitude and longitude.

I am sorry Bazetti was offended. He is such a nice fellow. He is only a third-generation Italian but he is more Italian than his own grandfather, who loathes Italian food and can't stand Bazetti's wine.

I can't blame him for not admiring Bazetti's wine. Bazetti makes a carload or so every year and Mrs. Bazetti, I guess, tromps on the grapes barefooted in the Bazetti basement. I am guessing this because her feet and legs are permanently red almost up to the knees. She doesn't go swimming because people stare.

It may be the resin Bazetti puts in his wine. His recipe comes from some part of Italy where the Greek influence is considerable. His wine is bitter. When you take your first tumblerful, your tongue rolls out like a busted window shade. After the first glass, you hardly notice. The way we do it, we all hold our noses with the first glass, then we push our tongues back with both hands, or a friend helps us.

The government once came around to see how much wine Bazetti actually made on his do-it-yourself permit. The government man tasted some of Bazetti's 1966, which was a vintage year, and he said Bazetti could make as much wine as he liked — because it certainly wasn't wine by any contemporary American standards. "The test," he said, "is whether it is drinkable, and I submit this is not."

CHAPTER IX

The Druids
and Father Ryan

There is a big rhubarb in our neighborhood at the moment because a couple of Druids moved in with four children, the Al Carters — he is Honest Al, runs a used-car lot downtown, "Honest Al's Used Cars." They may be the only two *practicing* Druids in the world, although a few English men and women interested in Druidism *do* meet once a year at Stonehenge to "observe" the summer solstice which was once the great Druid holiday, and there is scattered interest here and there in this country.

The Carters are not only Druids, but they are tithing Druids, which is the worst kind. This means they give 10 per cent of their income to the church, and this annoys the Income Tax people because the Carters are the only members of their particular church, and they pay themselves the 10 per cent for administrative salaries. But first they deduct the 10 per cent also as gifts to the church, and the Income Tax people have been going around and around trying to prove that the Carters' First Druid Church (of two members) is not an established religion.

When the Income Tax fellow came out to the Carters' to ask where the First Druid Church was located, Honest Al said, "It is located here, fella. You are standing on sacred Druid ground and don't you ever forget it."

And the fellow said, "I very much doubt that the Service will recognize this as an established religion. It looks like you are paying the 10 per cent to yourselves and then asking us to hold it deductible." And Honest Al said, "We are building a congregation very fast. We expect to have the whole neighborhood joining our parish before the year is out because our Sunday services will only be seven minutes long and there will be no sermon."

And the Income Tax fellow said, "Sheesh!" and the Service is still debating a ruling.

Mrs. Carter, who is a prophetess, second-class, in the Druid faith, said she and Mr. Carter had tried all the other religions and had found them wanting in one respect or another. Then they traveled to England two years ago and visited Stonehenge "and just fell in love with the whole idea." She read as much as she could find; there isn't much literature on the subject, really.

Mr. Carter lets his wife do anything as long as she doesn't monkey into his honest used-car business, and as soon as they decided to become Druids he put up a big sign downtown, "If you buy from me, your car will run forever — and you have my word as a Druid!" You've got to hand it to him. He says he figures if his religion isn't deductible as a religion, he can always deduct it as a business expense.

Al has these pictures up all around town of himself in a Druid bishop's suit, and it reassures people who are looking for good used cars because you expect a churchman, particularly a bishop, to give you the best possible deal.

Honest Al Carter's meteoric rise to bishop aroused some envy, and some anger, among the ministers of the more established traditional churches, to be sure. But as Honest Al Carter likes to say at neighborhood parties, it is wonderful to be a bishop and not have any clergy under you lousing things up.

Of course the Druid services in Honest Al Carter's living room every Sunday morning are supposed to be a big secret and all that the neighborhood knew about them (until very recently when Mrs. Fuller and Mrs. Dibble's mother joined) was that they last only about ten minutes and then they play bridge until late afternoon.

But by a curious set of circumstances, the Bazettis (of all people!) got to attend a Druid service last Sunday, and they are now telling one and all what happened. What the Bazettis witnessed certainly puts to rest those ridiculous rumors that Mrs. McMurty has been circulating that the Druids engage in wild orgies and sacrifice young virgins.

Of course I never believed this, anyway. Mrs. Honest Al Carter is too neat a housekeeper to permit orgies and sacrifices in her living room every Sunday morning. She is scandalized over the fact that The Widow is now wearing her neckline plunging down to here. This does not sound like a woman who would allow virgins to be sacrificed.

What happened was that the Bazettis went early to Father Ryan's church, before breakfast, and then Bazetti dropped by Honest Al Carter's house with a bottle of Marsala wine to show Honest Al Carter how to make a Marsala wine souffle. The way you do this is drink twice as much Marsala as you put into the souffle. Well, the souffle turned out beautifully, and Mrs. Honest Al Carter called Mrs. Bazetti to join them, so the Bazettis and the Carters ate breakfast together.

Then it came time for the Druid service and Mrs. Carter began to set up the bridge tables, and Honest Al Carter said: "No, no honey. How many times do I have to tell you, we can't set up the bridge tables until *after* the service?" And she said: "It just saves time, that's all."

Then Honest Al said to the Bazettis: "You might as well stay if you like. Mrs. Fuller comes in and the Dibbles' mother, and that's our congregation, and the service doesn't take long."

The Bazettis demurred saying they understood the Druid services were terribly secret, and Honest Al Carter said: "Well, we won't bring up any secret stuff today. We will make it very informal."

So the service started and all they did was sit for five minutes of silent meditation, then Honest Al Carter got up and talked about the depressed state of the used-car market, and that was it. Honest Al and Bazetti played gin rummy (which is pretty near as bad as an orgy, at that) and the ladies played bridge. During bridge Mrs. Carter assured Mrs. Fuller that she was including a prohibition against mixed dancing that Mrs. Fuller had demanded in the Druid creed and she also said that she was going to ask Father Ryan to help her with the wording. She expects to have the new creed finished by next Saturday — unless her cleaning woman fails to show again.

After the service the Bazettis got to wondering if they had violated their own church regulations by attending a Druid service and Bazetti asked Father Ryan. Father Ryan said he didn't consider the Druids a real church but more of an Irish club since the Druids have their origin in Ireland.

"I believe Honest Al Carter is a charlatan," Father Ryan told Bazetti, "but he is quite a good bridge player."

The whole neighborhood is in a ferment and I am counseling everyone to suspend judgment until the Internal Revenue Service rules.

*   *   *

The back of my hand to people who are intolerant and biased and prejudiced and like that. I mean, I even accept the *British.* I say they are as good as the rest of us, and I try to make myself believe it, and I bear them no resentment because they burned our White House and sacked our Capitol during the War of 1812. Long ago I forgave them for that, but I do occasionally recall with a twinge of indignation that they are the only major nation which ever invaded our country.

My friend and neighbor Father Ryan is not as forgiving as

I am. To him the War of 1812 happened last Thursday and he is still angry about it. He is forgiving in every other way. He can even forgive Honest Al Carter whom he believes to be an unprincipled charlatan. Whenever he thinks of the First Druid Church that Honest Al Carter started in his own home, Father Ryan holds his stomach and rolls his eyes and is really physically ill. But he has not yet, to my knowledge, thundered against him in the pulpit the way he thunders against the English.

I am an Episcopalian, and Father Ryan is not too happy about Episcopalians, either, because we are descended from Henry the Eighth through the Church of England. But he and I have worked out an amicable relationship. He is a model-railroader and I go over to the basement of his parish house and run his railroad. We meet on a hobby level if not on a spiritual level, and we get along fine.

The first time I met Father Ryan you might say he endeared himself to me by making a frontal assault on the British consul general at a party we were both attending. Father Ryan was polite as could be until the consul general, in a moment of appalling incaution, tried to draw Father Ryan out. He asked Father Ryan what he did for laughs, and Father Ryan promptly replied that he devoted his leisure hours (what few he has) to recalling to Americans that the British burned down the White House and sacked the Capitol.

The consul general treated this as a joke in rather lamentable taste, and then Father Ryan proceeded to convince him that it was no joke. Father Ryan wanted to discuss reparations and he thought negotiations might well start with a public apology from the current Queen of England. And until negotiations started Father Ryan was of the opinion that there should be no more commercial relationships between the United States and England, including Wales, Scotland, and of course, Belfast, which are the worst kind of English there are — he said. I didn't say it. He said it.

The consul general took it on the heel-and-toe between

the first and second highball, and I moved in to congratulate Father Ryan on his admirable handling of our common enemy. But he was wanting no part of me, either, until I told him I had 175 feet of HO track in my basement and we immediately left the party to see it.

Some of Father Ryan's English parishioners are disturbed from time to time by the way he inveighs against the English in his sermons. He blames them for almost everything — all the problems in the world today. "It's them dirty English," he says. I understand the bishop finally talked to him. The way Father Ryan reported the conversation, the bishop said he agreed with Father Ryan in principle but he thought fewer allusions to the English would make for a happier congregation.

But there is more than one way to skin a cat, and I understand now that any time Father Ryan preaches about Judas he quotes him in a cockney accent. The Sunday after the bishop talked to him, I understand, Father Ryan preached on the Last Supper, and when it came to the part where the Apostles were told that one of them would betray, Father Ryan quoted Judas as saying: "Gor blime me, guvnor, you don't mean me, do you?" It was a magnificent moment and I wish I had been there to share it.

*   *   *

Well, there are two more things I should tell you about the Druid Church. First, is how Father Ryan and Honest Al have made up. I don't mean that Father Ryan recognizes the First Druid Church. Father Ryan continues to brand Honest Al as a religious opportunist and a charlatan, but now he is also telling everybody that Honest Al is a rather decent fellow *personally*. I believe this is because Al disclosed to Father Ryan that the new Druid Church creed will have a paragraph denouncing the British.

The Paragraph denouncing the British will come immediately after the Paragraph denouncing mixed dancing which the church is putting in to please Mrs. Fuller who is, of course, one fourth of its total congregation so far. Father Ryan has no particular feeling one way or another about mixed dancing but he has strong feelings about the British.

I was at the Fullers' the night Father Ryan and Honest Al Carter reached their New Understanding. Father Ryan was being a bit difficult, I think. He said: "I am never quite sure how to address you. As Honest Al or Reverend or what." And Al said: "You might address me as Bishop because I am a bishop, you know." And Father Ryan said: "I am still amazed at how rapidly you progressed in your church, and with only four members." And Honest Al said: "That is the beauty of being associated with a lively, progressive organization. Promotion comes faster."

Father Ryan said: "I understand that your wife has just about finished writing your creed." And Honest Al said: "Well, yes and no. We have it pretty well hammered out except for the section denouncing the British." And Father Ryan said: "How's that again?" And Carter said: "I feel strongly that British influences on American life have been harmful and also I believe they are depressing the used-car market with stinking little English automobiles."

And Father Ryan said: "Bishop, I think I may have mis-judged you and I would be delighted to help with the drafting of the British section of your creed," and they walked away arm-in-arm.

The other development is that Mrs. McMurty is more convinced than ever that the Druids engage in terrible orgies and are dedicated to destroying the American moral fabric and raising the income tax and I don't know what. So she called a mass meeting at her house the other night to discuss what to do with the Druids. Honest Al stopped Mr. McMurty on the street and asked if he could come.

"Why certainly," Mr. McMurty said. "You are a neighbor and a good friend and this is a neighborhood affair, and I would be delighted to have you attend." Carter said: "I think it would be so much easier if I could hear firsthand what people are saying about me." And Mr. McMurty agreed: "It makes good sense to me. What do you drink?" Carter said: "American rye. I don't want any English gin or Scotch whisky because our creed is going to be against them."

Mrs. McMurty was furious when she heard her husband had invited Honest Al Carter to come to a mass meeting to protest him and his church. But she called Mrs. Carter and invited her officially and she is going to bring the coffee. I like to think this is the American Way.

CHAPTER X

The Fumbles

I've been thinking about clumsy women. I don't mean accident prone. I mean the kind of woman to whom things happen, unexplainably. Like they pick up a figurine in your home to admire, and when they set it back in place, carefully, it breaks. Or in a helpful way they go over to straighten a picture, and the picture falls and shatters. All this time the picture hanger has been half out of the wall, and the picture has merely been waiting for this woman to come along.

I mean the kind of a woman who graciously offers to help your wife with the dishes, and, boom! seven Lenox saucers! Or the kind of woman who always spills her cocktail down the front of her dress, or who backs up into the little table with the big potted plant on it!

There is a lady like this in our neighborhood and she is one of the nicest ladies I know, with a sunny disposition and a happy laugh, and is brilliant, actually. We call her Mrs. Fumbles. My prayer for all such ladies is that they be blessed with husbands as devoted and as watchful and as forgiving as Mr. Fumbles is. He follows her everywhere in public. And sometimes he keeps up a running commentary. "Now watch it, dear," he says. "Don't touch anything. Don't slam anything. There is no need to panic. . . ."

They've been married a lot of years now, and I think it is

interesting how it started. She had just dropped an expensive dish in this china shop, and the proprietor had become abusive, and Mr. Fumbles impulsively paid for the dish because the girl didn't have enough money with her and the proprietor was doubtful about taking her check.

"It could happen to anybody," said Mr. Fumbles, and she said pathetically, "It just seems to happen to me all the time," and she burst into tears, and he took her into his arms right there, and she has been in his arms ever since.

Before they were married he would go over to her house for Sunday dinner and help her with the dishes, and together they would run through half a set. To make her feel better he would try to drop at least one dish to her two. Her father and mother would sit in the living room with their hands clenched and their eyes would roll with horror as each crash came from the kitchen.

Her mother would say, "She doesn't get it from *my* side of the family. The clumsy ones are all on *your* side." And her father would say, "I do believe he is breaking dishes along with her to make her feel good. In my book that is true love." And her mother would say, "I can't wait until she has her own home to wreck."

But the funny thing is, nothing happens to her in her own home.

They have plastic dishes, for instance, and it's only when she forgets and leaves them in the oven a long time at high heat that anything happens to them. Even so, they don't actually melt. They just kind of lie down, tired.

And everything that could be knocked over is put out of reach or glued down. Her kids help a lot. They are responsible. They will say to one another, "We're going to play. It's your turn to watch Mama." And when she sets out for the supermarket, the oldest boy automatically calls out, "Checklist! Purse? Your distance glasses? Driver's license? Shopping list? And now remember, Papa says when you back out into the street, you put the car in reverse, not drive."

As soon as she arrives at the supermarket the manager immediately attaches himself to her and doesn't leave her until she is finished. They still remember how once she reached for a single can of tomato soup and the whole section fell over on her.

Mrs. Fumbles came over with her husband one noon to share our pastrami on date-nut sandwiches, and we ate in the backyard because it is murder to have her in the house. In the wintertime when you see her coming up the front walk, you rush around and put all the breakables out of her reach, and you place her in a chair that can be readily sponged off when she has gone.

First thing that happened was she was talking about how she hung a Picasso upside down because she liked it better that way, and she spilled her cocktail down the front of her linen dress. We had given it to her in a tumbler rather than a thin-stemmed cocktail glass because we are not stupid and there was a sizable amount, and it puddled in her lap.

She went on talking about Picasso and her husband said gently, "Dear, I don't want to alarm you, and I don't want you to rise abruptly and tip over your chair and the table here, but there is a small lake of Manhattan in your lap and down the front of your dress."

So she immediately arose and tipped over her chair and the table. There were several cats visiting us at the time and they enjoyed the pastrami immensely — and the date-nut bread, too, and I wouldn't have believed it if I hadn't seen it myself. She looked so terribly embarrassed and seemed on the verge of tears, and her husband put his arms around her and Green Eyes sopped her up.

Then Green Eyes took her inside and tossed her dress into the washer-dryer and gave her a hostess gown to wear until the dress could be ironed, and she came out happy and smiling again and caught the gown on a corner of her chair and pulled the sleeve off. But we all told her it could happen to anyone. It was the hostess gown I gave to Green Eyes for

Christmas, but she told Mrs. Fumbles she was going to send it to the Goodwill next week anyway. People will tell any kind of a lie to reassure Mrs. Fumbles. Mr. Fumbles was telling us he was terribly pleased with her because she won him the daily double — $1200 — at the track the previous Sunday. He had sent her to the window to buy a win ticket on No. 7 in the first and No. 5 in the second, and she forgot and reversed it and 5 and 7 came in to win.

Mr. Fumbles always sends his wife to the window. He says she averages about 61 per cent winners, and when you have a wife with a talent like that you can forgive a lot.

* * *

I don't know much about heredity. I don't know whether a clumsy daughter can inherit clumsiness from a clumsy father. Mrs. Fumbles' father was a widely-known customs inspector, old "Butterfingers" Benson, the fellow who dropped the Ming Vase worth about $30,000. His penchant for dropping almost everything he picked up was well known in Customs, and his superior said to him that day: "Now, Benson, I want you to listen carefully. I am going to send you down to the plane today to check luggage and anything the passengers may have brought from overseas. And I don't want you to touch *anything*. I want you to stand there with your hands behind your back, and let the passengers show you the stuff. And I don't want you to make any sudden gestures, knocking things off tables, you understand?"

And Butterfingers Benson said: "Of course I understand. I'm not a kid or something." And then, leaving the customs house, he fell down a full flight of stairs, but was only bruised.

So this fellow from the museum got off the plane with the hat box he had carried 9,000 miles on his lap, and there was this vase in it. And Butterfingers said: "You may hold the vase up for my inspection," and the museum fellow had it tightly held in both hands around the stem and raised to eye level,

and Butterfingers said: "A little higher, please, I would like to
see the bottom." And he moved his hand and pushed the vase
up, and it hit the pipe which supported a sign and suddenly it
wasn't a vase any more. It took a private bill in Congress —
this was years before the torts act — to compensate the
museum, and from that time on Butterfingers was assigned to
guard duty at the foot of gangplanks and on ships. Several
times he was carried away, but some pilot boat always went
out and brought him back before he was too many days out.

When he retired everyone said he was one of the nicest
fellows that ever served with Customs. They loved him, just
as everyone loves his daughter. At his testimonial dinner they
gave him a watch and chain, the chain so he couldn't drop it
on the floor, but it did drop into his coffee and break the cup
and saucer. He is still a legend around Customs, and they
wish he were still with them when they have to break up
contraband. With a sledge he was magnificent. He could
break up twice as much as men twice his strength and half his
age. And when he hit his foot or leg, it was never more than a
bruise or a very small break.

* * *

Mrs. Fumbles got into a terrible rhubarb in connection
with the PTA "Carnival" up at the neighborhood school. She
made some dirty gingerbread men for them to sell. Well,
gingerbread girls, too.

They weren't dirty, actually. They were realistic. I mean,
she made them nudes. She attacked the problem more as a
sculptor than as a pastry baker.

She is artistic, she is the most artistic person in our
neighborhood, she keeps us alert in the arts, and without her I
am afraid we would all be painting ourselves blue and living
in trees.

The PTA Carnival is an annual event to raise funds, I
think, to establish PTA missions around the world among

unenlightened people, and also to buy a new coffee urn. Everybody brings down stuff they don't want (and nobody else wants) to sell, or they bake cakes or cookies and like that. My mother-in-law, for instance, always contributes a half dozen plum puddings but they don't go very well because she boils them up in some of my old socks and they come out looking like feet. I have seen people turn pale just walking by them.

Green Eyes usually bakes a cake, using a mix, and if it turns out well she insists she made it from scratch.

Well, Mrs. Fumbles' children thought it would be nice if she would make gingerbread men for the PTA sale, and she made a project of it. She is a gay cook, and when she is flitting around in her kitchen it is like watching a ballet and what is on top of the stove is invariably of gourmet value.

She made fifty (count them — fifty) gingerbread men and girls, each about eighteen inches high. She could only get four in the oven at one time. And they were delicious and terribly interesting because she made them as primitives with sloping foreheads, prominent jaws, a very small brain pan, head growing right out of the shoulders, very muscular arms and a protruding abdomen.

The dullest person imaginable, furthermore, could tell at a glance which were the boy cookies and which were the girl cookies. Mrs. Fumbles' children were delighted but wondered if the cookies might be more acceptable to impressionable adults if they were clothed in white sugar trimming.

She would not hear of it, and she explained to her kids that there must be integrity in art, and there is no reason why gingerbread men and girls could not be artistic and it was time somebody faced up to the prudes and the hypocrites of this world. And the kids said okay, but Dorothy Leighton, the PTA chairperson, would blow her top, and they were right.

So Mrs. Fumbles called Dorothy Leighton and said she had fifty gingerbread men and girls that weighed two pounds each to get to the Carnival, and she needed a station wagon.

And Dorothy Leighton said, "I will drop by to look at them."

When Mrs. Fumbles took her into the kitchen where she had primitive gingerbread men and girls propped up everywhere, Dorothy Leighton's eyes hung out on her cheekbones, and she said coldly, "I am very much afraid that you are going to have to do a little altering on these cookies before they can be publicly offered under PTA auspices." And Mrs. Fumbles said she wasn't going to alter anything.

The whole neighborhood filed over to Mrs. Fumbles' kitchen that night to inspect the cookies, and we thought they were great. And we prevailed upon Dorothy Leighton to let them be sold at a table marked "For Adults Only."

Mrs. Fumbles sold all her cookies in the first ten minutes for two dollars each and took orders for two dozen more.

I am having the cookie we bought framed in a shadow box to be hung in our kitchen as an American primitive.

* * *

Terrible things happen to Mrs. Fumbles. She is an artist and she is the only one in the whole neighborhood who can tell you instantly *which* ear Kirk Douglas cut off. But you confront her with a piece of modern machinery like a coffee-grinder or an automobile or even a dustmop, why she has difficulty orienting herself to it. But the funny thing, she is a tremendous cook. Of course her husband and kids have to clean up after her, but they eat fine.

The other night her husband had some friends in for a little gin rummy, and along about midnight he went to look in the kitchen for whatever Mrs. Fumbles had prepared for them to eat. By this time she was upstairs in bed but she had just cooked up a great mess of stuff, and he was pleased to see that it was a casserole. Usually she leaves platters of celery stalks stuffed with crab meat, and fancy sliced breads and exotic cheeses and cold ham and like that.

The casserole was delicious and went down great with

cold beer, and the friends went home about one o'clock singing Mrs. Fumbles' praises very loudly. It is not every woman in our neighborhood who will encourage gambling and all kinds of evil by making a fancy meat casserole for the evildoers.

So the next day Mrs. Dibble called her to get the recipe. She said her husband had been utterly insulting and odious at breakfast asking her why she couldn't come up with exotic dishes like Mrs. Fumbles. And Mrs. Fumbles said oh, it really wasn't anything. It was just something she was experimenting with. She said as a matter of fact her husband had got the wrong dish. She had a cold lunch spread out in the refrigerator, but he had picked up the wrong food.

Then Mrs. Blair called to find out whether the dish was a stew or what, and Mrs. Fumbles was rather vague and said well, it was more like a ragout, and Mrs. Blair said did you make it by starting with a wine sauce? And Mrs. Fumbles said well, you could, but it really wasn't necessary, and then she dummied up.

So Green Eyes wandered over for coffee, and there isn't anybody in the world who can keep a secret from her, and she saw this book on Mrs. Fumbles' cookbook shelf — *The Secret of Cooking for Dogs* by Martin A. Gardner and she found the recipe on Page 22 under "Meat Surprise." Chopped meat, onions, carrots, diced celery, garlic, salt, tomato puree and crushed dog biscuit. It is the dog biscuit that makes it crisp and so heavenly.

Poor Mrs. Fumbles was about to burst into tears, but Green Eyes made a big thing of it and every lady in the neighborhood served something out of the book to her husband that night. Mrs. Blair served her husband a "Dogwitch," Mrs. McMurty served Mr. McMurty the "Meatball Soup" and cackled with delight when he asked for seconds, Mrs. Dibble gave her husband "Chicken Surprise for Canine Casanovas" which consists of chicken, egg, onion, celery and cottage cheese, and she told the other wives she couldn't see that it helped him any.

Fact is, they were telephoning each other most of the night and laughing hysterically, and it just goes to show that when you eat something tasty in somebody else's house you had better not go home and tell your wife about it because women will turn it against you.

I am lucky. Green Eyes gave me a dish for enceinte female dogs — leftover lamb, chopped bacon, minced onion and dog biscuits — but she substituted toast points for the dog biscuits and I take that to mean she still loves me.

*   *   *

The whole neighborhood is talking about Mr. Fumbles at the moment, and it is most embarrassing because I believe he is the first man in the whole of human history to get diaper rash after the age of forty.

He went to a doctor and that's what the doctor said, and he was pretty unhappy with Mrs. Fumbles there for a while because he believed it was her fault. Anything that happens in their family is usually her fault, and there was no reason to assume that this wasn't.

What happened was that Mr. Fumbles developed this rash, and Mrs. Fumbles looked up the name of a dermatologist and made an appointment for her husband to see him. But there was so much noise at the other end of the line that she didn't hear the doctor's receptionist clearly, and I guess the receptionist didn't hear her, either.

She got the right address, obviously, but she must have gotten the wrong suite number because when Mr. Fumbles showed up he found a waiting room full of haggard young mothers and kids pulling toys apart and shredding magazines, and one of the kids wanted to give Mr. Fumbles his security blanket (or at least let him chew on one end of it).

The receptionist seemed surprised to see Mr. Fumbles there and she asked his name, and when he told her that he had an appointment with the doctor, she said: "Oh, what did you want to see the doctor about?" And of course he wouldn't tell her. "I would prefer to tell the doctor," he said firmly, and she said: "I suppose it is something about one of your children, perhaps?" And he said: "I would rather discuss it with the doctor."

Well, pretty soon after a succession of young mothers had gone into and out of the doctor's inner office, pulling kids behind them, Mr. Fumbles was admitted, and he was surprised to find the doctor's inner office had dolls and teddy bears and a rocking horse. And he said: "Doctor, is there any chance I might be in the wrong place after waiting all this time?" And the doctor said: "It depends, I guess, on what you want to see me about." And he said: "Well, I have this rash and I can't account for it, and my wife got me an appointment here, but I am beginning to wonder if she hasn't fouled me up again."

And the doctor said: "Well, I am a pediatrician, but it is such a pleasure to have an adult patient for once, let me see the rash." So Mr. Fumbles showed him, and the doctor said: "Well, that is nothing more than our old friend diaper rash." And Mr. Fumbles said: "You must be kidding." And the doctor said: "No, actually, diaper rash and athletes' itch and a dozen other ailments are very closely related, and there is nothing very serious or even uncommon about this — except in the case of adults we call it by a fancier name."

And Mr. Fumbles said: "How does a fellow like me get diaper rash? I have no young children in my family, and I certainly do not wear diapers, ever." And the doctor said: "Oh, it could come a lot of ways. Too much detergent when your wife washed your underwear, or perhaps you got it by sweating or chafing. I'll write you a prescription."

So on the way out the receptionist wanted Mr. Fumbles' address, and he obliged but he would not tell her what he was being treated for. "Go ask the doctor," he said, "when I am a couple of blocks down the street."

Now most wives, if their husbands came home and said they had been diagnosed as having diaper rash, would fall down with hilarious screaming and laughing and slapping their thighs. But Mrs. Fumbles was terribly contrite when the doctor said the rash might have come from washing the clothes. She explained that the children had washed his underwear because she was still finishing her four-sided portrait of Joe Nietzsche, the delicatessen dealer down in the village. She is showing this picture soon, if she can ever get it done, at the Community Art Exhibit, and it shows Joe Nietzsche full-face both profiles, and also the back of his head. She is an artist with integrity and believes a portrait should show all aspects of a subject's head. The picture is Called *Portrait of a Pickle Vendor* and I am sure it will go right on to the All-City judging.

Mrs. Fumbles said: "Oh, I am so terribly sorry. Was he a nice doctor?" And he said: "He was the nicest doctor I ever consulted. He gave me a big all-day sucker on the way out."

Mrs. Fumbles told Mrs. Fuller about it, and Mrs. Fuller

told my mother-in-law, and when you tell my mother-in-law something it is like going on a network show. She gets around faster than Paul Revere.

Well, right after the Community Club meeting in the village last night, Mr. Fuller said to Mr. Fumbles: "I hear you are wearing diapers now, and every man to his tastes, I say, but tell me: how do you fold them?" And there were a lot of other crude masculine remarks like that, but Mr. Fumbles just smiled and never blamed his wife, and it shows he loves her very much.

* * *

The latest thing is that Mrs. Fumbles had a terrific inspiration. She was going to do a mural for the high school auditorium on *The Rape of Lucretia.* The high school orchestra a month from now is going to play a concert and do some things from the opera and she thought it would be nice if they played in front of a contemporary background — the music being contemporary.

I guess you know about Mrs. Fumbles' mural in our branch library, *The Rape of the Sabine Women.* It's very graphic and I believe we now have the only branch library anywhere in the world where kids under eighteen are not admitted unless accompanied by a parent or other authorized adult. I mean we have this sign outside our public library which says: "Minors not allowed."

And then she did the *Destruction of Sodom and Gomorrah* for the boys in the fire station, on the back wall of their locker room, and firemen from all parts of town and around the state come in on their days off to see it. Mrs. Fumbles built the picture around Lot's wife escaping from Sodom and looking over her shoulder and turning into salt. She is a rather buxom figure, loosely clothed, and the firemen regard her highly and they stand and look at the picture and say, "How about that!" and "She's *all* woman," and a lot of other expressions you hear in fine art critic circles.

Mrs. Fumbles works fast with a paint brush. One day Mr. Fumbles flew to Buffalo on a business trip, and when he came back the very next afternoon he found she had painted the whole terrible tragedy of the Titanic on the wall over the tub in the master bathroom upstairs. The ship appears to be sinking right into the tub.

Mrs. Fumbles went to see the principal of the high school where the kids were going to play, and she suggested she could whip up a very satisfactory rape in a week or two, and the principal said immediately, "Aren't you the lady who brought the dirty gingerbread men and girls to the PTA party?" And she said, "They were not dirty. They were merely unconventional. I baked them without any clothes, that's all." And the Principal said, "Exactly what kind of a mural did you have in mind for *The Rape of Lucretia*?"

And she said, "I thought I would have Sextus, the rapist, approaching Lucretia's chamber and Lucretia looking out the door with a look of terror and I intend to . . ." And the principal said, "Hold it right there. I can see where there might be some value in having the music students perform in front of such a painting, for one night only. But I don't think it would be good business to remind the youngsters every day thereafter, for heaven only knows how long a time."

And she said, "You forget the wholesome moral lesson in this painting. And I think you forget that before Lucretia killed herself, she swore her father and husband to avenge her. They chased her attacker over most of the known world." And the principal said, "I'm afraid the details have escaped me."

And Mrs. Fumbles said in despair, "Oh, I am afraid you are the kind of man who would want to put a pair of trousers on Rodin's *Thinker*." And the principal said, "If he were on *our* front lawn, he would certainly have to wear pants."

So they decided that she might try the mural, if she liked, with stick figures instead of flesh and blood figures, and she could portray this regrettable incident after the fact rather than before or during the fact. "I think it might be acceptable," the principal said, "if you had some stick figures chasing one another *after* the fact. I believe that would get the school off the hook."

So Mrs. Fumbles is doing some sketches but her heart really is not in it. She may never attempt the mural itself. In stick figures it loses its message. If she had done *Rape of the Sabine Women* and *Lot's Wife Fleeing Sodom and Gomorrah* in stick figures, I doubt they would be the great works of art they certainly *are* at the moment. All I can say is the high school has blown its opportunity to be one of the most talked-about high schools in the nation, but like Mrs. Fumbles told me, the path of true art is never smooth.

CHAPTER XI

The Blairs

Mrs. Blair has a terrible, unsolved problem, and it doesn't look like she can ever solve it.

The problem is that Mr. Blair spends almost all his time around home in the bathroom. He has a reading lamp there, and an ashtray, and a shelf of books, and even a portable TV. Of course, they have three other bathrooms. The fellow who owned the house previously built this huge powder room downstairs which Mr. Blair has sort of preempted, you might say, as his office away from his office.

When they were looking at the house, Mrs. Blair said, "Good heavens, Charlie, what would we ever do with *three* and a *half* bathrooms? I can see myself cleaning bathrooms all day long and never getting to the other housework." But a kind of a funny light came into Mr. Blair's eyes, and he said to the real estate man, "We will take it." And Mrs. Blair said, "You haven't even asked what the price is!" And Charlie said, "We will take it."

So they moved in, two adults and two teenagers, and Mr. Blair has been mostly in the powder room ever since. It's a big room, done cosily in rose and white, and there is a flowered cretonne-covered chair with arms, very comfortable, and Mr. Blair even keeps all his pipes and tobacco there, and two hunting rifles.

I tried to explain to Mrs. Blair once that the powder room in her house, and the multiplicity of bathrooms elsewhere, satisfies a deep psychological need in her husband. He was one of a family of fourteen, and when he was a kid he swore that if he ever found a bathroom unoccupied he would never leave it.

At the Garden Club there was this speaker who told about the effect of color upon human beings, and after the meeting Mrs. Blair asked whether there was any color that would drive a person from a room and make him uncomfortable and restless and like that. The speaker said certainly, dark blue.

So the other day Mrs. Blair had a paperhanger in and he covered the rose and white with two shades of blue, dark and darker, and the place looked like a tunnel, and Mrs. Blair said to the paperhanger, "What do you think of it?" And he said, "It's only for bodies. Leave me out of here to look at God's good green world outside again."

Mr. Blair came home and went into the powder room with two volumes of the encyclopedia, and he didn't say anything because Mrs. Blair is always changing the house around and he has learned in the past that it does no good to say anything.

But when they knocked on the door for him to come to dinner he looked peaked, and he said at the table, "I don't think I want much dinner tonight, I am beat. I just don't seem to have the old hustle anymore. I wonder if maybe I shouldn't retire and let the younger fellows take over."

The next day Mrs. Blair had a few witches in for lunch, and they each came out of the powder room saying, "Well, I give up. I've tried so hard but at last I am convinced there is nothing I can do for my complexion except slipcover it." And one lady said to Mrs. Blair, "You must excuse me dear, but I'm not feeling well. I've got these great hollows." And another witch said, "I look at myself in the mirror these days, and I know I am over the hill."

So the paperhanger is back at the Blairs' today. More rose and white wallpaper is going back and Mrs. Blair will still have her problem.

*   *   *

All the parents in this neighborhood feel guilty about their children. They are not sure they are bringing their children up right. They read books. They talk about it at dinner parties. Some of them are taking extension courses at night in psychology. Every time they scold a child or give him an old-fashioned order to straighten up and fly right, they are terrified inwardly. "Good heavens," they think, "am I marking him for life?"

The kids around here know this, too. A parent hollers at a kid who is sawing the house off its foundation, maybe, and immediately the kid begins to limp or develop a facial tic. Or he walks around with one shoulder pathetically lower than the other and looks rejected. The kids meet in one another's back yards and practice looking rejected.

Mrs. Blair the other night scolded her son for coming to the dinner table with dirty hands, and with great reluctance he retired and washed them. He shuffled away and came back with his head down. You could see he felt a great need for love and reassurance. In a split second he had become insecure. And when Mrs. Blair put down in front of him his favorite dessert, he quietly declined it, and she nearly burst into tears.

Mrs. Blair told Green Eyes about it. Green Eyes consoled her. "You think you have problems now," she said. "Wait until your daughter reaches her late teens and begins adolescent rebellion." And Mrs. Blair said: "She doesn't approve of me now. She tells me she is the only girl at school who has to clean her own room at home."

Green Eyes said: "They don't tell you about this when you walk down the center aisle on your father's arm in a beautiful white dress and veil, and say 'I do'."

And Mrs. Blair said: "I want to do the right thing. Do you think it is wrong for me to insist that Lindy help me with the dishes at night, and do a little housework on Saturday now that I'm working part-time?"

Green Eyes said: "I think you might as well make up your mind that anything you do at her age is going to be wrong."

Poor Mrs. Blair. What a shame that she cannot enjoy her renaissance unattended by child-raising problems. Her husband has fallen madly in love with her again since she got a job and a new haircut and some long false eyelashes to flutter at him and lost weight. He sits in his office and writes her torrid love letters, and calls her up on the telephone speaking softly to her, and runs all the way home from the bus stop.

And then her son won't eat his favorite dessert to punish her, and her daughter feels unloved because she has to tidy up her bedroom, and all the fun goes out of Mrs. Blair's life. It's almost enought to make her want to be plain and plump again.

Mrs. Dibble up the street has another problem. She had two children in her late twenties, and then heaven smiled again when she was forty-two. Now she drops off a daughter at college, a son at high school and another daughter at kindergarten. She faces the Girl Scouts all over again, and sometimes it unnerves her.

She tells Green Eyes that her elder daughter disapproves. She says subtle little things to her mother like: "Oh, Muth-er! At your Age!" And "What do people think when they see *me* and *her* going to school, in the same car!"

There is nothing in any of the psychology books to help Mrs. Dibble in her dreadful guilt. The two daughters get along fine. The older is, actually, very fond of her baby sister. As for Mr. Dibble, he doesn't feel guilty at all. He feels immensely vigorous and fulfilled. He's an extrovert, anyway, and goes through life pinching his cares away. I mean when he pinches ladies at parties.

*   *   *

Like I said, Mr. Blair has fallen violently in love with his wife all over again. It's nearly a scandal. The police caught them the other night down at the park. Sitting in their car at 2 A.M. looking at the moon over the frosted waters.

One of the cops said to Mr. Blair: "Who are you, fella?" And Mr. Blair said: "My name is Blair and I live up on the hill just a couple of blocks from here." And the cop said: "Well, maybe it is time you took the lady home and went home yourself." And he said it kind of nasty, and you could see he disapproved but he wasn't going to make a Big Thing of it.

And Mr. Blair said: "I am with my wife and I don't know any law that says you can't sit with your wife in your own car in a park you pay taxes for, and look at the moon."

And the cop says: "Look, fella. I am trying to be nice. So why don't you quit while you are even?" And Mr. Blair said: "This is my wife, and I wouldn't be sitting in a car at this hour with a woman if it wasn't my wife?" And the cop said: "Oh, sure. Now, wheel away before you get me sore." And Mr. Blair said: "I'll take you up to my house and I'll prove this is my wife."

And the cop said: "Well, I tell you what I am going to do there, Sporty. I'm going to call your bluff."

So the cops followed the Blairs to their house, across the street from mine, and went into the house, and the three Blair kids got up in their pajamas and identified Mr. and Mrs. Blair as poppa and mamma. And Mrs. Blair showed her driver's license and her house key and the wedding picture nineteen years ago and like that. And the cops were stunned.

"Might I make you a cup of coffee?" Mrs. Blair asked, and while she was doing it one of the cops went to the telephone and said: "You know that report some joker phoned in about a man and woman sitting in a car in the park? Well, Charlie, when I get back, have I got *something* to tell you!"

And the other cop said to Mr. Blair: "You folks been separated and then reunited, or have you been away a long time, or something?" And Mr. Blair said: "No, we have been married all the time. Doesn't every husband take his wife out once in a while and sit in the car with her?" And the cop said: "Well, frankly, no. This is the first time I ever heard of it being done. And I don't think it is going to catch on, neither."

Of course the cops didn't know about Mrs. Blair's renaissance. They didn't realize she had got mysterious along with it. They should have seen her before. I remember one Sunday when Mrs. Blair with her hair in the old style, coiled up and frayed at the neck, was pushing a rock as big as herself out of her rock garden. And Mr. Blair was sitting on the patio with a drink, and he said to me: "Chee-e, but is she ever clumsy!" That was before he fell in love with her again. Now when Mr. Blair runs home from the bus and she opens the front door, they embrace so hard that people across the street cry out: "Shame!" and "What kind of business is *that* for a family man!" and "Don't look now, but it is your own wife, you fool!"

I believe Mrs. Blair has been more of a good influence on the neighborhood, really, than The Widow. All the wives are sprucing up, and you ought to see some of the hair styles and eye makeup. Even Green Eyes said to me the other night: "I think I will try a new haircut. How do you fancy me?" And I said: "As far as I am concerned, I don't see any reason to change it." And she said — women say the darnedest things — "Do you still love me like you used to?" And I said: "We have a wonderful thing together, you and I. A nice quiet comfortable love and a priceless community of interest."

And she said: "Some lover!" What did she mean? Why did she get sore?

CHAPTER XII

The Bugle Lady
and Mr. Rabbitson

You remember the Bugle Lady, she is the gal who slips into her old Girl Scout uniform and steps out on her patio, usually about 2 A.M., and blows bugle calls to summon the neighbors to an early-morning buffet and a little booze for one and all. It used to be great fun to awake to the bugle and rush over to her house even though it did mean that you carried your head under your arm on your way to work later that same morning.

The Bugle Lady was always getting sore about something. Life bugged her, and when her indignation about something was more than she could contain, she'd let us share it. She was — and is — proud of the fact that she can still get into the Girl Scout uniform she wore when she was only eighteen and was the Scout bugler, and the wives around here hate her for it.

Well her husband, the dentist, inherited some property out in California, and shut up practice here and rented his home, and he and she went to California to administer the inheritance.

Now the Bugle Lady is back. She didn't tell anyone she was returning. She wanted it to be a surprise. One night we heard the bugle. At one o'clock in the morning. "Boots and Saddles" with an off-to-Buffalo finish. She really swung it.

I sat straight up in bed. "It's Mrs. Paul Revere!" I shouted.

"The British are coming again! Nobody else in the world today plays bugle like that!" And Green Eyes said: "Oh, no. No. No. No!" About twenty of us gathered. I got there in a dead heat with Mr. McMurty. Mrs. McMurty was behind him,

and I don't think she'd had time to get into a girdle because instead of being 40-40-40 straight up and down, she looked more like 40-48-40. The Widow, the Dibbles, the Coopers, the Fullers, the Blairs were there, and Mr. and Mrs. Jack brought over his cannon to fire a welcoming shot. Happily, he forgot the powder.

I mean everyone had their arms around everybody, and all the men, at least, had their hands around a glass, and there was chicken a la king bubbling in a chafing dish on the sideboard, and toast points, and I don't know what else.

The Hixlys were there, too, and Mrs. Hixly immediately enrolled the Bugle Lady in her campaign to Legalize Brown Rice, and Mrs. Peterson told the Bugle Lady how the President was reading her mail and listening in every time she talked by telephone with her sister, Agnes, in South Dakota. It was homecoming. It was like the Old Grads getting together once more.

This time the Bugle Lady didn't have too many things to complain about, just too many ding-a-lings in California. Basically, she is a malcontent. It starts with her resenting the fact that nobody ever stands up in a public auditorium and says: "Is there a dentist in the house?" and there is never a dentist as hero in a TV series where he's really a secret agent who drills right through a molar into a nest of microfilm. She carries on a continual vendetta with doctors' wives because they speak of the Bugle Lady's husband as "doctor" in a patronizing way. They don't give him credit for being as much a doctor as theirs.

We broke up about three. There was a little argument about who was going to take The Widow home, but Green Eyes and I did it. The Bugle Lady's husband, the silent type, didn't say much but he seemed pleased to be at home. I tell you, the neighborhood is going to pick up real fine now. I think it will begin to swing again.

The Bugle Lady's husband is highly respected in our neighborhood and is doing wonders for Mr. Rabbitson, one of the most difficult cases around here, mentally as well as dentally.

Mr. Rabbitson brought me over a pair of Indian moccasins last Thursday, and they are lovely. So soft. He made them himself. He chews the leather until it is quite pliable. He read in *National Geographic* that Eskimo women who chew leather have jaws like wire-cutters. It is quite an experience to go to his house for a formal dinner and see him chewing a moccasin during the cocktail hour, between sips of his martini. He does it to strengthen his jaw and keep his teeth healthy. He has this *thing* about teeth.

Mr. Rabbitson, I guess you might not remember, is one of those who missed out during the great college toothpaste test.

He was short-changed. He belonged to the group which got the toothpaste without the magic ingredient. He came home with 38 per cent *more* cavities than anyone else. His mother rejected him. "Other kids go to college and come home with better teeth than when they went away," she told him, "but you got to come home with a mouth full of holes." He tried to explain that he had no choice. He had been taken into the test and had innocently thought that he was one of those who would be benefited.

His mother said to him: "I'll tell you one thing. If your father had taken that test, you can be sure he would have got on the right team. But you, no!" And he said: "But, Mom, they didn't tell us! We all thought we were getting the same toothpaste!"

Shortly after that, he began covering up his mouth with his hand when he was in public. It came on shortly after his marriage, a real psychosis. "Why do you cover up your mouth?" his wife would ask him. "Because I don't want my teeth to fall out," he would say.

Actually Mr. Rabbitson has no cavities now. The Bugle Lady's husband understands his problem and isn't annoyed when Mr. Rabbitson rushes in three or four times a week to ascertain whether a new cavity is developing.

Dr. Spook, our friendly neighborhood psychiatrist, has done a lot for him, too. Mr. Rabbitson was going to another psychiatrist there for a time. This fellow was tracing the whole disturbance back to Mr. Rabbitson's initial rejection by his mother. "You really wanted your mother to *approve* of your cavities," he said. "You wanted her to be as proud of you with your cavities as other mothers up and down the block were proud of their sons with 38 per cent less cavities."

There may be something to this theory, I don't know. I have met the older Mrs. Rabbitson when she was visiting here, and she is not basically mean or vindictive. She is only stupid and you can't blame people for being stupid. You can only blame them when they are proud of it.

The older Mrs. Rabbitson *is* a perfectionist, and she wears her hair in a tight bun on top of her head. I believe at one time she also had her cheeks pierced for bones. She says things to her son's wife like: "I did so hope that my son would marry well," leaving the implication that he didn't. And young Mrs. Rabbitson, who understands her mother-in-law very well, says cheerily: "Oh, shut up, Mother," and they get along famously.

Well, when Dr. Spook got the case he sympathized with Mr. Rabbitson. Dr. Spook usually refuses to take patients whom he knows socially, but this case fascinated him. "I don't go for this mother rejection stuff," he told Rabbitson the very first session. "Your trouble is — and I am going to use a very precise professional term — you have what we psychiatrists call a 'bird on the head'."

He persuaded Mr. Rabbitson that there was nothing personal in being chosen for the wrong group. "Life is a lottery and you lucked out. You ought to feel sore about it, not beaten and rejected. Get good and mad." And Rabbitson said: "Grrrrr!" And Dr. Spook said: "That's more like it."

He persuaded Mr. Rabbitson that the toothpaste company was a big, soulless corporation that didn't give a fig whose life they blighted. "Write to them and demand equal time on television for people in the test who got more cavities," he advised. "Get a lawyer and sue them. Fight, fight, fight."

So now Mr. Rabbitson chews moccasins and is very much better.

*   *   *

I often lie in bed at night worrying about how my tongue keeps out of the way when I am eating or talking, often both at the same time. I should never have done it, but I mentioned this worry to Mr. Rabbitson. His wife now tells me that he stews all day long, and well into the night, over how his tongue knows when the teeth are about to bite it and gets out of the way. She says he bites himself two or three times at each meal and blames me for it.

Mrs. Rabbitson said in a fury to Green Eyes: "My husband hasn't been able to think of anything else. Every mouthful he's afraid he's going to bite his tongue, and he does, too. Never before has he bitten his tongue and now he is biting it continually."

Green Eyes said she's sure I didn't do it intentionally because she woke up the other night to find me sitting straight up in bed and when she asked why I was sitting up I said I was worrying about how my tongue knows to stay out of the way of my teeth when I'm chewing. And Mrs. Rabbitson said: "I wonder if there is a husband in the whole wide world who isn't nutty about something. First, mine chews leather, now he's keeping track of his tongue." And Green Eyes said: "It's our cross to bear."

Dr. Spook went by the house the other night when I was watering the lawn and said: "You had to go tell Rabbitson about the tongue getting out of the way of the teeth and he told me, and now I have bitten myself twice. . . ."

CHAPTER XIII

Grandma

Some people have pores that don't open and close the way they should. Like my mother-in-law. Her pores sometimes stick half-open and half-closed, and it is a real problem, not only for her but for Green Eyes and me.

I wish newspapers and magazines would quit printing stories about how open pores keep you cool and healthy in hot weather and closed pores protect you from cold in cold weather. Every time Grandma reads something about pores, her own pores begin acting up. I try to tell her that she is suggestible, but she denies it. She says she can feel that her pores have been malfunctioning for years, and they often stick halfway between open and shut.

She comes down in the morning to breakfast and says: "Well, my pores are open today, and I know I am going to catch my death of cold." And I say to her: "How do you *know* your pores are open?" And she says: "I just know, that's all." And I say: "A person doesn't have any control over his pores. Nature opens pores and closes pores according to the body's needs. It's an automatic system." And she says: "Well, this morning they are stuck open, and that's all there is to it!"

This means I have to run about the house tightening light globes in their fixtures, and taping the electric utility outlets in the walls. Grandma believes — and I can't find any scientist to refute her — that electricity leaks into rooms from loose light globes and from wall outlets that are not plugged with tape. She says these electrical currents are instantly drawn to open pores, and once in your body they shoot through a person's liver. In time, if your pores admit enough electric current, your liver turns to jelly.

"Well, there we go," she will say suddenly, pressing a hand to her abdomen, "there is an electric draft somewhere in this room, and I can feel it already in my liver." We used to be able to get the doctor over to treat Grandma's pores when they stuck open or stuck shut, but now when we call him and tell him electrical currents are piercing her liver, he just says: "Pull the master switch and bring her in to see me in the morning." This means we've got to sit around in the dark.

I tried once to show Grandma a cut-away of the human body, and how the body consists of a skeleton overlaid with successive layers of muscle, tissue, and fat. And I showed her how the organs are distributed through the body. She rejected this concept even though it was in a recently-published encyclopedia.

She prefers her own concept of the human body, which is that the body is a skeleton covered with skin and filled with clockwork from which a pendulum slowly swings from side to side, turning gears, cams, and wheels. If you bend over too long, the pendulum stops and you are in bad trouble. Occasionally she will stand in a doorway and swing a bit from side to side to speed up her pendulum, and I have tried it, and the surprising thing is that it does help. I don't personally believe the pendulum part, but something *does* click inside. And if I do lean suddenly forward something bumps against the inside stomach wall.

This latest pore difficulty is due to a published piece saying that clogged pores bring on prickly heat and malaria and sudamina and chestnut blight and I don't know what else. Grandma read that you've got to keep the pores active and clear. When they get clogged, why you've got to stop using strong soaps and greasy ointments, and you should spend "from eight to ten hours in an air-conditioned room" for perhaps ten to fourteen days consecutively.

We don't have air-conditioning in our house, and that means that Grandma will have to sit in some cocktail parlor for eight to ten hours a day, for ten to fourteen days, and I don't believe any cocktail parlor is going to let her. You see, she is against drink. She is even against beer. Any time she sees someone drinking beer she sings a song about how she won't let the brewer's big horses trample *her*. It's a real swinging song, but it cuts down beer consumption something awful.

She also walks through cocktail parties around the neighborhood saying: "Liquor Kills" and "How many drinks does that make for *you* this evening?" I don't know *where* Grandma can sit while her pores recover.

For years Grandma has complained that television was shooting rays through her liver. She felt it mostly when she was watching programs that Green Eyes and I liked but that she didn't much care for. She has *never* felt the rays shooting through her liver when she watched Lawrence Welk or other cultural shows of that nature. For years she has been sitting off to one side of the set to avoid rays and then the United States Public Health Service confirmed that some dangerous rays really do come out of *color* television sets!

Of course, we don't have a color set yet. When I want to see a baseball game played on red grass I go over to a neighbor's. Once during the last World Series the grass changed three times in one inning, and I had trouble following the ball because it was flesh-colored when it left the bat, turned green (over red grass) in the infield, and was a bright blue when it bounced off the back wall in far left field. I kept thinking how difficult this must be for the players.

The rays that shoot through Grandma's liver came from our black and white set, and we still may have the only black and white ray-shooting set in the country. The Public Health Service says you should never sit closer than six feet from *color* television, but they don't mention black and white.

My grandchildren used to stand with their noses pressed to the very screen of our black and white television, and they never afterward complained of pain in their livers. I used to wonder why they stood so close, and I discovered one day they were actually watching the actors on the sidelines before they appeared in the picture.

I pressed my own nose against the screen one night when my granddaughter, Elizabeth, was pressing her nose and looking sideways, and doggone if I didn't see the Marshal standing there with his horse, talking to some floozie, while a decent woman on the screen was being attacked by Indians and hollering for help. The Marshal just stood there with the floozie until it was time for him to come into the story.

On another occasion, Elizabeth, with her nose pressed to the glass, called out that Cher was walking around offstage in her flimsies waiting for a change of costume, but I didn't look. Cher is a nice girl and I like the way she sings, but I haven't the slightest wish to see her in her flimsies. One night, on the other hand, Sophia Loren was in a TV show and I posted Elizabeth to watch around the corners of the screen and to holler if Sophia Loren walked around in her flimsies, but she never did.

Television is very real to my mother-in-law, who is eighty-five and has difficulty sometimes in disassociating real-life from make-believe. She becomes part of the action herself. She talks to TV. "He's right behind that rock!" she will cry out as the Marshal rides openly and incautiously into Box Canyon. And when the villain invites the innocent country girl up to his apartment to share a quart of bourbon, Grandma says: "Don't you go, dear. Don't forget that nice young man waiting for you at home." As a matter of fact, often the characters in TV stories will respond to Grandma, and come down front and look at her directly and say: "Thank you, ma'am."

Well, Grandma has something new to worry about these

days. My wife hates plastic and all its uses in this modern world, and she likes to say at cocktail parties that one day the Russians will invent a ray which, with the press of a single button, will cause all the plastic in the United States to disintegrate. Grandma heard Green Eyes say this, but the way she understood it is that the Russians have *already* got such a ray.

"The Russians have this machine where you press a button and all the plastic in the United States will melt," I heard her telling the milkman, and he was stunned. "Did you just hear that on the radio?" he asked, and she said: "Oh, no, they wouldn't let the radio say that because people would become panic-stricken. But my daughter knows all about it."

My mother-in-law has been right so many times that I am scared, too. I even believe what she says about fish being a brain food, and that night air is poisonous.

*   *   *

I want to tell you about taking Grandma to the horse races. She loves horses, and the reason I don't take her to the races more often is that she hollers pretty loud to bring her horse in ahead of mine, and she uses a good deal of body English in the stretch.

I grubstaked her this time with a ten-dollar bill and she came home with the ten and with twenty-eight more, betting show all the way. I mean, to net twenty-eight dollars on show is about as good as you can do anywhere, so I let her keep the ten, too, because I am a Big Man.

I wish I could explain my mother-in-law's system but it defies explanation. It's got something to do with jockeys. She goes to the paddock before each race and studies the jockeys' faces intently, and she tells me what she is looking for is a kind of spiritual quality. I have been around a few jockeys from time to time, and I have listened to them talk in their more casual and unguarded moments in the tack room, and I do not believe I have yet detected any appreciable spirituali-ty. But I guess I don't know what to look for.

Grandma will look them over before a race and she will finally fix upon the most dejected in the bunch and she will say: "Now, *there* is a nice, clean young man and he is going to win!" And I will protest: "To me he looks like he has been up all night and before I would lay even a two-dollar show ticket on him I would want to see his saliva test."

And she will say: "No, he's a fine young man." So she bets on the horse he is riding, which has no chance whatever, and I bet on the horse I *know* is going to win, and her horse romps in.

So we are sitting at this table near the window in the Turf Club and Green Eyes and I are averaging out the handicap-pers, and the horses parade by on their way to the post, and Grandma is studying the jockeys through a pair of two-dollar binoculars, looking for spirituality. And this friend comes along who owns horses and knows horses better than they know themselves. And he says, like he is telling me the secret of the hydrogen bomb: "The word is out. It's Little Choo-Choo." And I say: "Is this the one to beat?" And he says: "Will go today." And I say: "Looked good last time out?" And he says: "Now or never." And I say: "Is he ready?" And he says: "Can do." And I say: "Are you on him?" And he says: "A bundle."

And I say to Green Eyes: "I believe I may put a buck or two on Little Choo-Choo because my friend here, who knows all about horses, says he is ready. Also it would be kind of a hunch bet because I am also a railroad fan and model-rail-roader and a horse named Little Choo-Choo wouldn't let me down."

But Grandma likes Sigh Lotti because the jockey has more character in his face than anyone, and Sigh Lotti wins and Little Choo-Choo comes in fifth after stopping in the far turn to inquire the way to the men's room.

So I saw this friend who put the bundle on Little

Choo-Choo and he seemed extraordinarily jolly for a fellow who had lost a bundle and I tried to cheer him up. I said: "I need you like I need smallpox. What can I pay you to stay away? I should listen to Grandma."

And he said: "I know, I know. She touted me off on the way to the window. She's got something going on jockeys. I win big on her horse."

* * *

The horse-racing season is over now and many of the horses I bet on this year are snugly wintering in their kennels. I mean, most of the horses I bet on wag their tails when you speak to them, and a few want to get right up in your lap. I once asked an old horse-player how you tell a horse from a dog and he said you have to catch them in some intimate moment in the paddock. If a horse being paraded around the paddock halts momentarily to sniff at a bush, don't put any money on him, he's a dog.

Horses talk to me, but it is no help at the mutuel window because I find they invariably lie to me. Very few horses will tell the truth. They will look you right in the eye and tell you they are ready, they are the one to beat, they have plenty speed, but it's lies, all lies.

I talked to a fine-looking colt named Date With Ali. "How's it with you?" I asked. He said: "I'll be right up there at the wire." And I said: "But you haven't won since August." And he said: "I may be ready for upset." And I said: "But you're running against On The Muscle." And he said: "I just missed in last." And I said: "You're ready?" And he said without faltering: "Might go this time."

My friend the president of the track came to me with a good horse, but he said he had been touted off it on the way to my table. I said: "Never mind. I have just been talking with Date With Ali and he says he Will Make Them All Run." And the president of the track, who is a great judge of horses, said:

"That's good enough for me."

So Date With Ali came in eighth in a field of nine and he just shrugged when he passed me. My friend the president asked: "Is there anything we can do to make your visit more enjoyable?" And I said: "Yes. Leave me go out on that track and kick Date With Ali right in the belly."

Racing is good for a lot of people, however. I firmly believe it brings a lot of people *outdoors* who would never step outdoors for anything else. The last time I was at the track, I encountered at least three persons suffering from the bends. The fresh air was getting to them.

Well anyway, after this disastrous meeting with Date With Ali I went home and tossed all night and had this terrible nightmare where I found a bottle and pulled the cork and a genie came out. The genie said to me: "You have three wishes, ask me anything." And I said: "I need only one wish. I want you should give me a horse that will always finish two lengths ahead of all the other horses no matter what kind of a race you put him in." And the genie said: "You must be out of your head. If I could come up with *that* kind of a horse, do you think I would spend any more time in a bottle?"

CHAPTER XIV

The Children

Let me tell you about the neighborhood children who took valuable things to Show-and-Tell at the Aaron Burr Elementary School recently. The youngest Blair child took his father's and mother's marriage license and little Timmy McGarrity took $10,000 worth of Burlington Northern Preferred and Gulf Oil stock. The Burlington Northern Preferred amounted to only ten shares at about $7 a share and was Timmy's, the rest was Gulf and his father's.

I am not quite sure how the Blair child got hold of the marriage license but the way I hear it, Mr. Blair is continually and roguishly asking Mrs. Blair if she is sure their marriage is legal and if she has the license to prove it, and on the last occasion she produced it, and they both looked at it fondly and left it on the living room table. Old Mrs. Crump, the second-grade teacher, was horrified when the Blair kid stepped up to the front of the class to exhibit the license and she rushed it to the principal's office for safekeeping. The Blair kid told the class, "Papa is always saying he will take Mama down to City Hall some day and get her properly married, and it is some kind of a joke."

Mrs. Blair had to go to school the next day and recover her marriage license, and she said to Mrs. Crump, "I wonder if you are not perhaps putting a little too much pressure on these children to show and tell something interesting when nothing really interesting has happened to them?" Mrs. Crump said she had been holding show-and-tell sessions for twenty years and this was the first time a child had ever brought along a marriage license. "It is almost," she said, "as if he were worried about the legality of your marriage and his own position in Society." And Mrs. Blair said, "Oh, don't be ridiculous. He is just a resourceful and imaginative little boy." But I guess at the teachers' lunch table they talked about nothing else.

The stock was a good deal more serious. McGarrity talks to his child at dinner about stocks and the market and capital gains and depletion allowances, and the kid knew what a debenture is before he was being read Mother Goose. He is enormously proud of his ten shares of B.N. Preferred and is permitted to keep the certificate in a lockbox in his own bureau at home.

The McGarritys went east on a trip and left their children in the care of Mrs. Lucretia Borgia. She caters widely around the neighborhood, and she and her husband, Cesare, do some baby-sitting, too. While the parents were absent the mail brought an envelope from McGarrity's broker in New York and inside the child found the Gulf shares.

He took both his and Daddy's shares to Show-and-Tell and I understand that the teacher had palpitations as she hurried them along to the principal's office. The principal kept them in his safe until school closed and then rushed them downtown to the big safe in school headquarters, leaving a note at the McGarrity home where they were. He did talk to Mrs. Borgia, but he soon discovered that she is about as bright as she cooks, which is not much and not good. She just thought the stock was kind of pretty. McGarrity will be home tomorrow. If there is a lot of screaming at his house you'll know what it's about.

*　*　*

I used to play and romp with my children sometimes. I don't mean taking them out door-to-door tricking and treating on Hallowe'en Night. I used to do that too, when mine were small, and people would say: "Well, goodness! What have we here?" And my children would say: "Twick or tweet." And they would receive some candy and I would just stand there, and people would say: "Who is this big goblin with the horrible mask?" And I would say: "It is my natural face and I will thank you to keep a civil tongue." And they would say: "Would you like some candy, too?" And I would say: "No. I would like a martini." A fellow can get loaded that way in just two or three blocks.

I used to try to play games with my children at other times, but frankly, I don't think they really wanted me. Green Eyes would say: "Why don't you go out and play with your children?" And I would say: "They are playing Indian. How can I play Indian? I don't have a suit." And she would say: "Couldn't you put a single feather in your hair and be an Indian?" And I would say: "Some Indian! A single feather!"

It was easier to play with my daughter, Marybeth, and her friends, but it was costly. They always made me the daddy with the money. They would say: "Daddy, I must have some money to go to the store," and I would never get the money back. Girls learn early.

I also went to little-girl teaparties. But when little girls make tea out of old tea grounds and water from the garden hose, they expect you to drink it. You can't say just "yum, yum" and pretend you are drinking. They know when they are being patronized.

I used to play baseball with my son Charles' sandlot team and there was always a good deal of argument as to which side I would join, and the losers got me. When I came up to bat, my own son would try to bean me. He would throw one of the hard ones and I would go home with a turkey egg on my head, screaming for the witch hazel, and I'd hear the kids say: "Well, we can play now."

When my grandchildren visit us now, I say in the jolliest way I can muster: "Let's all go out and play hide!" But nothing. They are watching Star Trek on TV, with men rocketing out into space, and their eyes are bugged out on their cheekbones.

I say: "Come outdoors and I'll show you how to make a whistle out of a fern stalk," and they don't even answer me.

* * *

Green Eyes bites little children.

The way it happened, my grandson and namesake, Douglass, was visiting us and so was his sister, Mimi. He is two and a half and she is one. He bites her and makes her cry. While Mimi was having her lunch out of the rooster plate in the high chair and minding her own business, Douglass approached and bit her arm. You could see tooth marks. She screamed.

Green Eyes took him aside and explained that people didn't go around biting other people. She said brothers *loved* little sisters. She said it hurts when a person bites a person. She explained all this beautifully, I thought, and he seemed to be attentive. But I said to her: "I will give you 'A' for effort, but I will also give you five to one that he does it again."

So he did it again. And Mimi cried again, and the tooth marks again were deep. So Green Eyes bit little Douglass and it was his turn to cry. "That's how it feels," she said. "That's what you did to Mimi. When you bite Mimi, you hurt Mimi." I don't think Green Eyes bit him hard. I could see no tooth marks when he came flying to me. She bites me a good deal harder.

"Now you did it!" I said. "The kid will grow up remembering all his life that his grandmother bit him. All the nice things you have done for him he will forget. All he will remember is that you bit little kids."

And she said: "That's the way I stopped my own children

from biting. I suppose there is some enlightened method today using applied psychology, but I don't know it."

And I said: "The little beggar will go out now and tell everybody in the neighborhood that you bit him."

And she said: "Oh, don't be absurd. You dramatize everything."

So he went across the street and told old Mr. McMurty, and later, when Green Eyes was walking Douglass around the block, Mr. McMurty said: "Your grandson tells an incredible story. He says you bit him and you bit his sister, too."

And Green Eyes said: "Children are so fanciful at this age."

She not only bites little kids but she won't own up to it, either. Her life is a tissue of lies and evasiveness. Mr. McMurty is a retired banker and you don't fool him easily. He has X-ray insight, and he sees through people right into their evil, seething hearts.

He told her: "My wife used to bite my kids, too."

* * *

Ordinarily I don't have much contact with bogeymen but my small granddaughter, Mimi, is visiting us at the moment, and she is conditioning herself both to bogeymen and monsters and Frankensteins. She knows exactly at what time and on what stations bogeymen and monsters appear on television and she yells pretty loud unless you produce them for her. And then she stands with her back to them and only occasionally glances over her shoulder.

She is a blonde and I suppose she already instinctively knows that when she gets to be oh, around eighteen, twenty, some shaggy beast as big as a house will reach through her bedroom window with a hairy arm, pluck her out of bed in her sheer silk nighty, and carry her away, kicking and screaming, through fog-shrouded streets to some dreadful fate.

This is the Violence Age of Television, as you already know if you have been watching the nasty thing, and all my grandchildren are responding as expected. Willie, who used to keep law and order in Dodge City, Kansas, as a two-gun United States marshal, is now wrecking his model cars in wild chases; his sweet little sister, Elizabeth, is sawing rubber dolls in half and shrieking with delight.

My other grandson and namesake, Douglass, is nailing plastic men to boards, and his hair stands up in terror like a fright wig. I got him the little men to shoot down decently with a slingshot, but no, he's got to nail them.

I have difficulty at the moment communicating with my wife. She has been taking care of Mimi while her mama, Miramae, and my son put in a lawn at their new house. Mimi's manner of speaking has rubbed off on her. I always snort when I hear adults being warned against talking baby talk to children. I know for a fact that it goes the other way. Children corrupt adults.

The other night, to give you an idea, Green Eyes inquired whether I had wound all the tick-ticks. A moment ago she called upstairs to tell me my num-num was ready. Last night at dinner she admonished me to eat up all my nice meatsie-meats, and later she inquired whether I wanted both tookie and iceteem.

But this is nothing compared to the way Mimi's baby talk gets to my mother-in-law. To give you an idea, right after breakfast yesterday, apropos of nothing, my mother-in-law inquired whether I had gone toi-toi yet, and I told her savagely I didn't consider it any of her ever-loving business and that the question was an unwarranted invasion of my privacy.

I find it easy to talk to Mimi in a quiet conversational tone and in everyday English. Her face lights up with pleasure when I tell her that dogs go meow, meow, and that cats go bow, wow, wow, and that horses go quack, quack, quack and that ducks go kut-kut-kawdawket. She knows Pa

Doug is funning.

But my mother-in-law is disturbed. "You can't tell her that dogs go meow, meow, meow," she says. "Why, the poor little girl will grow up to distrust her grandfather."

And I said, and I think it makes good sense: "The best thing she can ever learn is that she can't trust *any* member of this family on either side."

And I do not talk baby talk to her. Ony dess an itto bit.

* * *

Two of our grandchildren have been staying with us while their daddy and mother are in California hunting a new home to go with a new job. Up comes an important birthday for Willie, his twelfth, and Green Eyes said, "I must take him back to his old neighborhood and give him a birthday party with boys he knows." And I said, "Fine, I'll go with you." And she said, "I don't think you are up to it. It can be gruesome, and it can be awfully noisy." And I said, "I can handle it." Elizabeth, his sister, who is eight and very worldly, said warningly, "Boys' birthday parties are not as nice as girls' parties because girls are quieter." And I said, "That's female chauvinism, and don't be undercutting your brother on his birthday." And she said, "You'll find out."

Well, we drove up to a rendezvous in the old neighborhood and two of the kids were waiting — they had been there since early morning, I think. But the third kid was late because, it turned out, he had failed to tell his mother he was going to a birthday party until he was leaving home. His mother had to drive to the shopping center (and back) at roughly eighty miles an hour to pick up a present he could give my grandson, and I believe she was a little put out because when the boy arrived half an hour late at the rendezvous he was saying how difficult mothers are sometimes and what an uproar they make over the most trivial things.

So off we went to a restaurant that caters to kids' birthday parties, and to the movies. Green Eyes drove and Elizabeth sat primly beside me in the front seat and the four boys sat on the back seat. Well, "sat" isn't the word, exactly. They "wrestled" on the back seat; they were opening the presents and letting paper and string fly out the window, and I was screaming about littering.

I had forgotten that four twelve-year-olds could make that much noise. I kept turning to the back seat and saying, "Okay, okay, now knock it off," and Elizabeth pressed my knee and said softly, "I told you."

The restaurant is a kind of Gay Nineties place with Funny Signs around, and it specializes in ice cream with a few hot dishes, and it is The Place To Go for Birthday Parties. I said, "Well, I guess everybody wants a hamburger, hey?" Well, yes, they wanted the hamburger grilled with cheese, bacon, with onion and lettuce and French fries — at $2.50 each. I muttered to Green Eyes, "Aren't the little beggars satisfied with plain hamburgers?" And she said, "You're buying for a gourmet crowd."

Elizabeth got a hot dog, a Whing Ding Special, with chopped lettuce, tomato and onion and mayonnaise, cost only $1.75, she loves her grandfather and doesn't want to see me sitting on the poorhouse porch.

Let me tell you about the desserts. One of the boys had a Union Station Woo Woo consisting of vanilla, chocolate and strawberry ice cream, banana wheels and a "marvelous smoke stack topped with fruit, whipped cream, slivered almonds and cherries" at $2.25. The other three chose the Gibson Girl which consists of vanilla ice cream, a nonalcoholic grenadine, a "banana nectar from the tropics," topped with whipped cream, "exotic sherbets" and toasted almonds. At $2.45 a copy. A stinking sundae for $2.45 *each*!

Oh, I forgot the root beer. And the sides of sauerkraut. I watched them shovel this stuff away and I said to Green Eyes, "We're not taking them to the movies. We're driving them right to the emergency ward at the nearest hospital." And when the check came I said to her, "Do the little beggars eat like this when they go out with their own folks?" And she said, "Hush. It's a birthday party and there's a difference."

The movie was a Horror picture, it scared me worse than it did anyone else. These terrible creatures suddenly loomed up out of the night. I covered my eyes and said to Green Eyes, "Tell me when they are gone." I barely made it through to intermission, and then discovered the whole crowd had to be provisioned again at the candy counter. I said, "Do we have any insurance that will cover us if their parents sue?"

I spent the time after intermission outside the theatre, just walking up and down, enjoying the quiet zephyr-like noises of ordinary traffic — automobiles honking, brakes screaming, fenders crumpling, anything to get away from the pandemonium in the theatre when the monster was eating the blonde, with a knife and fork.

I thought the theatre was the end of the birthday party. But no, they had to go through something called the Fun House where they were tipped and tilted and shaken and dropped and frightened silly. We got them all back home before they showed any visible signs of illness themselves, and we got the grandchildren home and they weren't sick, either.

But I was. Oh, brother, was I ever indisposed. At nine o'clock it hit me and Green Eyes held my head, and Elizabeth looked in and said sweetly, "I told you. All boys' parties are like that. Boys are just too rough and make too much noise, I always say." Next time I will listen to her.

*   *   *

My grandchildren, Willie, twelve, and Elizabeth, eight, who are now living in far-off California, write me a couple of times a week, big, long, informative letters, crammed with news, and I am going to tell you how I arranged it.

I pay them half a cent a word, not including, however, the salutation or the signature. But I do pay half a cent for "love" if they sign with love.

I don't know if I would recommend this to you or not. The half-cent rate does smoke out the letters, but it is costing me about four dollars a week. The little beggars are writing about everything they see and hear. Perhaps I should have set the rate at a quarter of a cent per word. I set the half-cent rate one night when I was feeling bad that they were going away and after two double martinis. It goes to prove again that one should never enter into any financial dealings when one has had two double martinis.

Elizabeth has a little trouble writing as fluently as her brother, but she knows I like trains and the Western Pacific main line can be seen from their home, and she is not beyond listing every car of a hundred-car train that passes her house. I get letters from her, "Dear Grandpa Doug. The Western Pacific went by today and they had cars from the New Haven, the Southern Pacific, the Great Northern, the Tidewater Southern . . ." and so on fifty cents worth. Still, I am hearing from her. She tells me about her dolls (twenty-five cents worth, and about how Mama Got Mad at Papa (thirty-two cents worth) and how much fun it is in school (eighteen cents worth) and like that.

You don't realize how observant children are, how much they see and retain of family life and its small and large crises until you have a couple of paid informers working for you right in the bosom, you might say, of that family. Nothing escapes my bright little spies. Their mother wrote me that her husband had bought her a nice new coat. But her children wrote me and told me what it cost!

My daughter said casually one night in a long-distance telephone conversation that it had rained in Stockton one day and that her new house, far out in the country adjoining a golf course and tilled fields, had filled up with field mice. She just said there were a lot of mice around, and that she had called her husband, Dick, to report that they were crossing the living room rug in platoons. And she said that her husband had been assured by old-time Stockton residents that mice always go into houses when it rains.

But my grandchildren, writing for half a cent a word, described later how Mama had hysterics and wanted to call the county sheriff's office, and stood on a chair. Willie was enchanted by the mice and he professed to recognize some of them, and he gave them names at half a cent a word. The mice that came into my daughter's house in Stockton one rainy day cost me a good two bucks.

I'm right in there. I know what the family eats for breakfast and dinner and what the youngsters are carrying to school for lunch. I know that a fixture in one of their three bathrooms flushes with a sound very much like a diesel locomotive horn. Their daddy is trying to fix it, but I don't know why he should. I would love to have a bathroom fixture that sounded like a choo-choo when you flushed it. It reminds me that when I was Willie's age our bathroom had a ceiling-height flush tank with a long chain-pull. I used to lean out the window and pretend I was an engineer on the New York Central running into Toledo, and I would pull the chain when I came to grade crossings. It was my whistle cord. I would have been out of my mind if a train whistle sound had resulted. Willie is lucky and doesn't know it.

There are 900 gopher holes, Willie writes, on his school ground, and an average of two gophers lives in each hole. He sees gophers on his way home from school, and the other day one little beady-eyed fellow let him get within a foot or two before he vanished down his hole. Gophers so far have cost me $1.12. Maybe in the years to come the grandchildren may do better in English composition than other children who haven't grown rich by writing letters to their grandparents.

My other grandchildren are now in Los Angeles. Douglass II, my namesake, six, and Mimi, going on five, write to me but not on a paying basis yet. Douglass' letters are mostly drawings of what he is doing with a little printed text, and Mimi's are stick figures and scrawls, and it is pretty hard to put a price on drawings and scrawls. But they will soon be demanding equal pay with their cousins and my overhead will go up.

If you decide to follow this system with your own children or grandchildren, perhaps you'd better set the rate at a quarter of a cent. I have here on my desk now a letter from Willie about cable cars in San Francisco and it is going to cost me $2.80!

CHAPTER XV

The Women

The ladies of the Investment Club meet at my house once a month, and you never heard anything like it.

They are not like the ladies of the Garden Club who can be quite gay at times and who near drive me crazy, when I am upstairs trying to work, with their chatter and their peals of laughter over nothing. The ladies of the Investment Club are more like grim and foreboding, and when they like something the best you get out of them is a titter. Mostly they view with alarm.

I was listening at the top of the stairs to what their president, Dorothy Leighton, was saying, and I went down to remonstrate with her. She said coldly: "The ladies of the Garden Club may not mind that you listen to their meetings at the top of the stairs, but I feel that our Investment Club meetings have a more confidential character and I would be pleased if in the future you would curb your curiosity when we are here."

And I said: "I like to hear what you are buying because then I know what *not* to buy. You have a genius for buying and selling the wrong stocks at the wrong time, and it has helped my own investing considerably."

Shame on me, I shouldn't have singled her out but she is the predominant voice in the Investment Club because (1) she started it, and (2) she can holler louder than any of the others.

My broker, Sam Insull, was out to talk to them briefly. He told them he liked utility stocks, and then he opened up a chicken and studied the entrails and told them what the market would be doing the next week. He went away with an order for three shares of one stock and one share of another, and I don't think his brokerage fee even paid for his gasoline, and certainly not for the chicken which Dorothy Leighton took home. She won't share anything with anybody.

And then the biggest rhubarb broke out you ever heard. You see, the ladies had bought three shares of Phillips Petroleum, and along came this nice warm, friendly, mimeographed letter from the president, welcoming them into the august company of Phillips stockholders. Dorothy Leighton read it and the ladies beamed and said he was a nice, polite man and it reassured you to know that your money was in a company run by a nice, polite man.

But then Dorothy Leighton showed a gasoline credit card which the president had thoughtfully sent along to her. Well actually, he made it out to the Dorothy Leighton Investment Club because that is the club's name. I guess he was confused, because his letter was addressed to "Dear Mrs. Club."

So Mrs. Fuller got up and said she wondered whether the club would be obligated to pay for Dorothy Leighton's gasoline if she charged it on the card. Dorothy Leighton said Mrs. Fuller was being gratuitously insulting, and she resigned right there, and was going down the front walk, putting on her coat, when they called her back.

And then Mrs. Thorndyke wondered if they should change the name of the club to just plain "The Investment Club" and Dorothy Leighton put her coat on again, and they had to call her back a second time. So I went down and suggested that the club write to the president and ask him for a credit card for *each* member, and that settled it. They had a wonderful time forming a committee of the whole to draft the letter.

Ladies who belong to investment clubs had better remember that investment clubs are usually joint venture partnerships, and must file annual partnership returns to the Income Tax people showing dividends, interest, capital gains, losses and like that. And they must have a number.

I didn't know anything about this until a gentleman asked if the Dorothy Leighton Investment Club had a number and was duly registered with the Income Tax people. He said: "If it is run like all other women's investment clubs, they have done none of these things. . . ."

Well, I hate Dorothy Leighton because she is the bossiest woman I ever met, and she hates me, too, and for a time after I got the inquiry I had these wonderful daydreams where Uncle Sam slapped her right into jail for ten or fifteen years. I mean I would sit around the house and smile widely, and Green Eyes would say: "What's the reason for the big stupid grin?" and I would say: "I don't have to tell you everything just because I am married to you, you know. I can have secrets and wonderful thoughts without sharing them." But she finally got it out of me. "Dorothy Leighton," I said, "may very well be on her way to the federal bucket."

Green Eyes was horrified. She said she was a member of the Dorothy Leighton Investment Club, too, and the government might consider every member to be an offender, and I said: "I think they will only prosecute the officers when I inform them." And Green Eyes said: "You will not inform on us! And I am an officer. I am in charge of coffee and salad." And I said: "I don't believe the Income Tax people would pull in a woman who was only in charge of coffee and salad."

Well, Green Eyes went right up to Dorothy Leighton's house with the news and Dorothy Leighton said: "That's what comes of letting the investment club meet at your house and have your husband listening at the top of the stairs!" And Green Eyes said: "How much do you estimate the club made for each member last year?" And Dorothy Leighton said: "I estimate that we made twenty-nine cents in interest per member, and $3.68 in capital gains. But you must remember that the market fell off last year."

And Green Eyes said: "If we only made about four dollars a member in interest and capital gain last year, I do believe the Income Tax people would forgive our overlooking the law, and assign us a number." And Dorothy Leighton said: "You don't know the Internal Revenue Service."

Mrs. McMurty, who is the treasurer this year, was furious with me because the way she understood it over the telephone was that I had already turned the club in to Uncle Sam. Green Eyes couldn't persuade her different. "I will have Mr. McMurty get in touch with our Senators immediately," Mrs. McMurty said, "and put a stop to this nonsense."

McMurty called me that evening. "I hear you are fixing to send my wife to jail," he said. "How soon do you think it will be? Can I count on it?" I mean, the McMurtys have an odd marriage. But they do have a community of interest. They can't stand one another.

The only similarity between the Garden Club and the Investment Club is that they both eat the same kind of dessert, a foot high and mostly whipped cream, and I don't know why they don't fall dead on my front lawn on the way home. The clubs meet at my house because Green Eyes has the largest coffee urn in the neighborhood, and what with the coffee and the drinks and the luncheon, it costs me pretty nearly fifteen dollars a meeting. The ladies are supposed to contribute to the luncheon cost but mostly they forget. But if they would pay up their proportionate share of the meeting expenses — and their prorated share of Mrs. McMurty's cakes — why, I believe each of them would lose all their earnings each year.

I would hate to see some poor Income Tax accountant trying to figure the value of one of Green Eyes' fancy salads and those sticky drinks she makes, and I don't think the best accountant the Internal Revenue Service ever had could come near figuring the cost of Mrs. McMurty's cakes. Like I say, her fillings are marmalade and whipped cream, and brandied cherries and whipped cream, and when a lady eats a slice she goes into a stupor for three days.

* * *

A fellow told me the other day that he has been eating lunch at home lately because he changed his job and now often goes to work in the mid-afternoon. He had seldom before seen his wife eat lunch and he was astonished to see that while she set the table for *his* lunch, she seemed to prefer to stand at a kitchen counter to eat her own.

He inquired about this strange behavior and she said, "Oh, you know, I always eat on the run." Well, at a few neighborhood parties I have been asking other wives how they eat lunch, and I find this is rather common. I was working for a while on the theory that standing while eating lunch was a kind of self-imposed martyrdom, but now I believe the reason some women stand while eating lunch at home is that they feel lunch is really not worthwhile sitting down to.

One lady said to me, "Every time I look in the refrigerator to see what I can scrape up for my lunch, my stomach rolls over. I would not dignify my usual lunch by setting the table and sitting down to it. Generally I am gnawing on the bone left from the roast two days ago, or I am eating the pudding some child left last night, or I am heating up some of the leftover vegetable from last Tuesday. Now, lover, would you be a prince and get me another drink? . . ."

Although my neighbor Hixly, across the street, eats lunch often at home, his wife will not eat with him. She sets a plate for him in the kitchen, but she eats her own lunch in the living room off the coffee table. I was over there one day and noted this, and I said to Mrs. Hixly, "Are you people finally separated?" and she said, "Oh, shut up," but it turned out that she had been eating her lunch in the living room for years and she was not about to change her routine just because her husband had retired. I said to her, "Why don't you let him bring his plate in here with you, then?" And she said, "He spills."

Mrs. McMurty finds out what time her husband wants lunch and then she has her own lunch at another time. He is retired, too, and mostly she sends him downtown. She told Green Eyes, "I loathe eating lunch with my husband. Of course I also loathe eating breakfast and dinner with him as well, but I loathe lunch most."

I eat lunch with Green Eyes often, and she sets the table for it, and Mrs. McMurty has blundered in a few times when we were eating lunch together and has said to Green Eyes, "I don't know why he can't go downtown for lunch like a decent husband would." And Green Eyes says, "He works at home." And Mrs. McMurty said, "Well, if it were my husband, I would put a stop to that in a hurry!"

Mrs. Dibble says she eats lunch standing up and that she would not want Mr. Dibble to eat lunch with her because there is too much danger of being poisoned. You see, Mrs. Dibble's mother saves all the leftovers and wraps them up in dozens of little foil packages. She cannot be broken of this practice and sometimes these packages go unnoticed a week or two. Mrs. Dibble opens them at arm's length (sometimes they explode) and examines them and throws them away.

"Mother will even save six Boston baked beans," Mrs. Dibble says, "or a single Brussels sprout, and I cannot get her to date her little packages or write on them what they contain, and my refrigerator is crammed with them. If my husband were here, there is no telling what he might get and he is not as cautious as I am."

And I asked Mrs. Dibble, "Does your mother ever eat any of the stuff she puts away in these little leftover packages?" and Mrs. Dibble said, "No, never. She merely saves the stuff. I can't get her to throw anything away that is edible."

Mrs. Fumbles has no sense of time, and often Mr. Fumbles will come home from work and find her just finishing her lunch. "Why good heavens," she will say, "are you home early? I am just having lunch." And he will say, "Do you realize it is quarter of six?" She stands up, too, for lunch, but she does it so that she can do her stomach exercises between bites. She compresses the muscles of her abdomen and then slowly lets them out. It works pretty good, too. She has the waist of a schoolgirl, but that may be due also to the fact that three or four times a week she forgets to have any lunch at all.

I have often wondered what fun women can possibly have going to women's luncheon parties and I have concluded that it is because they have such miserable lunches at home that they are delighted to sit down to a well-served lunch in someone else's home. Mrs. Fuller was just over to have Green Eyes pin up her hem, and I asked her what she had for lunch and she said, "I had four boiled onions left over from last night – while my husband undoubtedly is right now eating short ribs of beef and apple pie at his club!" I am sorry I asked her. She clouded up like a thunderstorm.

*   *   *

I think you will agree with me that something has got to be done to stop these crazy women in my neighborhood. They are all "junking" at the moment. You know what that means. In just the last week Mrs. Peabody has brought home an old plow, Mrs. Phillips has brought home a barrel of horseshoes and Mrs. Honest Al Carter has brought home a church bell.

Mrs. Peterson is currently collecting commodes. And Joe Nietzsche's wife – he runs the village delicatessen and is quite a philosophical fellow – is collecting brass cuspidors which she converts into planters. She's got them all around the entrance to the delicatessen and they give a nice green touch to the place, but Joe has to move them all in at night and out again in the morning, and on very cold days he has to keep them inside. Mrs. Nietzsche drives up to a hundred miles on her junking trips, and Joe figures these planters cost him about forty-seven dollars apiece. It's a good thing Joe is a philosopher. He says, "I would rather have her running all around the state to junk shops than sitting in some bar making eyes at young fellows while I am working hard here slicing up pastrami."

Joe Nietzsche is a very sound fellow and his only fault is that sometimes he pinches ladies while they are leaning over his pickle barrel. But the ladies around here consider that to be one of the natural hazards of buying pickles, and his pickles are well worth it. If you let him pick out your pickles, why you don't get the best ones, at the bottom of the barrel.

Mr. Phillips got off the bus the other night and came down the street and saw his car sitting right down on its rear wheels and the trunk lid open and a barrel of something inside. He went into the house and said to Mrs. Phillips, "What the heck have you got in the trunk this time?" Only he didn't say "heck." And she said, "Isn't it wonderful? I got a full barrel of horseshoes!" And he said, "What the heck are we going to do with a barrel of horseshoes?" He didn't say "heck" the second time, either. And she said, "I thought we might nail them all around the porch and paint them different colors, artistic-like." And he said, "Are you out of your ever-loving mind?" And she said, "Who else around here has a barrel of horseshoes?" And he said, "Who else *needs* horseshoes?"

I must say, they may not be so artistic, but they are definitely arresting. And they are rather in keeping with the Phillips' house which is the oldest around here. The house was the first in this development and the original bathroom was about 150 feet behind it, up a pretty steep hill, which was murder to climb on a windy night or in a blizzard.

Mrs. Peabody found her plow at a country junkyard and she, too, came home with the rear of the car riding on the tires, and it took Peabody and two other men to lift it out. She's got it scraped and sanded and painted white in her front yard. People say to Peabody, "My, how interesting! What is it?" And he says, "It is an old plow painted white. What it is doing on my front lawn you will have to ask my wife because I haven't got the slightest idea." And they say, "It must mean something." And he says, "I will tell you what it means. It will mean that this summer I won't be able to run the lawnmower straight across the yard. It will mean I will have to clip the grass by hand all around the stinking thing."

But as Joe Nietzsche told him, "It is just one of the little penalties a man has to pay for living with a Good Woman."

Mrs. Honest Al Carter's bell, though, has the whole neighborhood aroused. She found it in a junkyard and paid pretty near $200 for it. You can hear it for nine miles. She has it on a wooden bench in her front yard, she rings it at 10:45 A.M. every Sunday morning for the First Druid Church services.

It is one thing to have a bunch of quiet Druids filing into church across the street or next door, but it is quite another thing to have a bunch of noisy Druids ringing a church bell. Mrs. McMurty, who lives next door to the Honest Al Carters, insists the Druids sacrifice young virgins, and when she hears the bell she says, "Well, they are sacrificing another virgin," and Mr. McMurty says, "I wonder where they find them."

There is talk in the Community Club about taking legal action against the Druids because of the bell. On the other hand, they don't seem to mind the phony carillon in our neighborhood church, which is just a record and sometimes gets stuck, or the needle gets dull and the bells are fuzzy. If there is anything I can't stand it is fuzzy church bells.

While we are on the subject of "junk" I've got to tell you about the rummage sale we just had and how all the ladies are sore at one another, and I believe it would take only one more rummage sale to split Our Society right down the middle.

This sale was put on by the Hospital Guild at the Legion Hall and it was quite a social event because the Guild is about as high as a lady can go socially around here.

I began to suspect that something was not quite right with the rummage sale when Green Eyes gave a rather nice epergne to the sale the night before it opened — and I saw one of the committeewomen, Mrs. Fuller, walking home with it later that evening. It never even got on sale. Mrs. Fuller was on the pricing and marking committee and saw it first. The reason I didn't like it is that the handle is bent a little and two of the glass dishes are missing and Grandma has been putting birdseed cups in their place. Grandma brought this epergne when she came to live with us and it reminds her of the old days. But it always has irritated me to see the birdseed cups in the epergne and one night I said I wouldn't eat dinner any more if the crummy thing stayed on the table and Green Eyes decided to give it to the rummage sale.

The question is raised, is it ethical for the ladies on the pricing and marking committee to gobble up the best goodies themselves? Well, Mrs. Fuller was victimized herself, you might say. She brought down her elephant's leg umbrella stand. Mr. Fuller told her to get it out of the house. It was too much of a temptation for his pointer, Wetter. To Wetter, one of the stupidest dogs I ever knew, an elephant leg is an elephant leg whether it is being used to hold umbrellas or not.

Mrs. Fuller's umbrella stand never got to the sales floor, either. Mrs. McMurty priced it and marked it and then promptly bought it. And she priced it at only six dollars! Shouldn't an elephant's leg umbrella stand bring more than that? I mean, even if it is slightly used and needs a good airing?

The Widow put in a charming frock with a designer label, in excellent condition, and you know what another member of the pricing and marking committee did? Mrs. Cooper, she bought it for her cleaning girl! A beautiful dress, The Widow paid over $200 for it and said she wore it only through one winter. Green Eyes was over at The Widow's and saw the dress and said it was in beautiful condition and that

The Widow had had it dry-cleaned. I asked Mrs. Cooper why she had not put the dress up for bidding or something, and she said why didn't I mind my own business. She said no decent woman in the neighborhood would dream of buying anything The Widow had worn. She is another of the wives who are afraid The Widow is fixing to run away with some husband around here.

Mrs. Cooper, in turn, gave that big plate she had with the picture of a dog wearing glasses and smoking a pipe and reading a newspaper. It is very choice. She got it at the World's Fair in New York. Here again, a member of the committee grabbed it before it ever could go on sale and fetch a big sum. Mrs. Peterson now has it hanging in her breakfast nook and says she loves it.

What happened, as you can see, was that all the best stuff was glommed onto by the committee and never got to the public. I have never been able to understand rummage sales. It seems to me that a rummage sale is a place where people give stuff they don't want (and maybe even loathe) and buy stuff they shouldn't want, and which is equally loathsome.

Mrs. Dibble gave her husband's whole great collection of girly magazines, which he has been saving and indexing for years. He didn't know and was furious. None of the women would buy them, either, and they finally were given to the boys at the village fire station.

I worry about this a little. The next time the fire bell rings I wonder if they will get away as fast as usual.

*   *   *

I sometimes wonder what it would be like to have a second wife and have to adjust to a whole new set of idiosyncracies and wiles. So the other evening I strolled across the street and asked Mr. Hixly. I don't know how many wives he has had and I suspect he has to count up, too. But he seems happily married at the moment.

He was planting moss and chickweed and dandelions in his lawn so his would look like the rest of the lawns around here and he said: "Why hello there, Neighbor Welch. Did you come over to see my soap collection again? And I said: "I saw it once and that's enough forever."

And he said: "I just received a whole new set of Western International Hotels, in mint condition." And I said: "I am very happy for you, but what I was wondering is: what is it like to adjust to a new wife? Do you make comparisons with past wives?"

And he said: "Certainly, man. That's half the fun."

And I said: "I am thinking about the really important *major* things which determine whether marriage succeeds or fails. Does she snore and how does she cook and does she wear old worn-out pants around the house and does she grab the bathroom first when you're getting ready to go to bed, and like that?"

And he said: "Well, the wife I have now — let's see, her name will come to me in a moment. . . ."

And I said: "Hetty." Hetty Hixley. Some name!

And he said: "Oh yes, Hetty. I want to tell you one thing, Welch. You've got to be careful never to call a new wife by a last wife's name."

And I said: "I'll remember."

And he said: "The thing about Hetty that is different is that she is queer for vegetables. I am a meat-and-potatoes man myself, and my other wives never tried to get vegetables into me. But Hetty won't give up. I get two vegetables a night and if I don't eat them I get them next day in salad or soup. Tonight I had broccoli in cream with chipped beef. I hate broccoli but I had to eat it to get at the chipped beef. I seem to get more leftovers with this wife than the others. I suspect that every other day she cooks for two days."

And I said: "That's a sneaky trick lots of women do."

And he said: "I think the big difference about Hetty is she loves to run around in the morning dew on the lawn in her nighty and robe and in bare feet. I suppose you've seen her out before breakfast with the dog? I'll tell you a secret. The dog doesn't have to go. She uses him as a cover to draw up the strength of that good earth and grass into her feet. I guess you'd call her an ecologist."

And I said: "There has been some talk about it."

And he said: "Oh, I've had better cooks, all right, but the thing about Hetty, she is crazy about helping me catalogue my soap collection."

Then The Widow walked over and slipped her arm through mine and asked what we were talking about and, since she's been divorced three times, I asked her whether it was difficult for a woman to adjust to a new husband and she smiled and said: "They're all nice."

So I went home. I had been talking to Hixly fifteen minutes and to The Widow thirty seconds and Green Eyes said: "Well, I notice you had a nice long talk with The Widow this evening."

CHAPTER XVI

The Men

Some of the men in the neighborhood have carpools. You know how it goes, each member of the pool has a fixed day. For instance, Jim Dooley drives them in on Monday and Tom Barnes takes them in on Tuesday. Only Tom's car is laid up at the moment and Jim Dooley has to take them on Tuesday, also.

On Wednesday it is Jake Bower's turn, but Jake's wife needs the car and Jake is one of those finks who has only one car, so they go in Jack Barnes' car. But Jack's turn normally doesn't come until Thursday. On Wednesdays, you see, he can't leave town as early as the others, so they hang around in bars until he is ready to go. Jack can't drop his passengers in front of their homes; he has to help them up onto their front porches and get a receipt from their wives for their safe delivery, and he has to explain to each wife just how it happened.

Now comes Thursday (Jack Barnes' regular day, but he did his stint on Wednesday, remember) so it's up to Jim Dooley to step in again, but he's in New York on business and the Friday man substitutes. I don't know who the Friday man is, but I can tell you what happens sooner or later on Friday, or some other day: the car draws up to its destination, the pool members step out, each draws a revolver, they begin shooting, and when the smoke lifts, everyone is dead.

Something like this happened to one of our carpools this week. Mr. Fuller announced that he would never let Mr. Cooper ride in his car again because whenever he comes to a railroad crossing Mr. Cooper shouts: "Railroad crossing coming up!" And Mr. Fuller said he would never let McMurty ride either, because when McMurty leaves the other fellows in the city he invariably says: "Well, don't take any wooden nickels."

On the other hand, Mr. Dibble claims that Mr. Fuller *offends* by eating raw onions for breakfast. This is not true. What Mr. Dibble detects is the odor of raw sliced onions in the brown paper bag Mr. Fuller takes to his office for his mid-morning "health snack." Salted raw onions, he says, keep his blood thin. I suppose his practice of eating onions at 10:30 A.M. is well-known around his place of business, and the only reason he hasn't been fired is that he is the president and nobody seems to object.

The other member of the pool is Hixly. He is always late and comes flying out of his house with a piece of heavily buttered toast in hand. The pool regards him coldly and merely grunts when he salutes them with his customary, cheery, "hello." He climbs in and pinches a few knees and says: "How's it with all you finks today?" and they say: "Oh, knock if off," and "Don't bug me," or "Quiet is requested for those still sleeping."

What broke up the pool the other day, Cooper got out right after Fuller crossed the tracks in front of the Commuter by only five feet and broke the gate on the opposite side. Cooper said, his face contorted with rage: "I hope there is another war because if I am ever offered a choice of going to war again or riding in a carpool, I'll chicken out and go to war."

When McMurty got out at the end of the ride and said: "Don't take any wooden nickels," Fuller, who was still trembling from the close call at the crossing, looked out with a face full of loathing and said: "What are you, some kind of a flipping parrot with a key in your back?"

The wives are planning to get the boys together and reassign them to other pools. Meanwhile they will have to drive their husbands to work and they say this is the greatest horror to which a wife can be subjected.

*   *   *

A lot of men in the neighborhood take regular exercises because Exercise Is Good For You.

About half a dozen of my neighbors have rowing machines now. I have one and I find the best time to row is when television commecials are on. I watch the program and the minute they break for the commercial, I am rowing like mad, and I get something like ten minutes of rowing every hour. I also row when the program gets dull, or when there is a love scene where the hero is smothering the heroine with kisses, that's a good time to row.

My friend Mr. McMurty, across the street, has a bicycle. Not a real bicycle. It's just the front wheel, and where the rear wheel should be is a metal stand. He pedals the bicycle against friction and it also has a speedometer.

Mrs. McMurty loves the concert hour on the educational channel and she becomes pretty bitter when Mr. McMurty, who also loves the concert hour, brings his bicycle into their TV room and starts to ride it in the middle of a symphony. The trouble is he calls off the speeds he is traveling, and when he has pedaled a mile he calls that off, too.

There is a grave question in my mind whether the exercise bicycle is doing Mr. McMurty any good. He often stops for a cold can of beer, and he tells me the bicycle really is no help in getting a person's weight down. He says he has gained seven pounds since he brought the bicycle into the house.

Honest Al Carter has a rowing machine like mine, and his wife told me the other night she would leave him if he ever rows through a Lawrence Welk waltz again. Carter replied he couldn't stop in the middle of the lake. He is a man of great imagination, and he stages these races with himself on the rowing machine, and as evidence of how fair he is, he tells me he often races an imaginary opponent and *loses*. While Welk was waltzing, Al was winning, and he was not about to drift in his rowing machine while some imaginary opponent overtook and passed him.

My friend Mr. Dibble, up the street, has neck trouble, and his wife got him a contraption which you can hang over an open door. It's like a bosun's chair for your head. There are straps that fit under your chin and over your head and a weight that pulls and you can put yourself in traction. He sits with this on when he watches television, and Mrs. Dibble says it is very hard for her to concentrate on a program when her husband has elongated himself too much and is turning blue. Dibble claims he has already gained one inch in height and I wouldn't be surprised.

Mrs. Dibble's mother watches television sometimes with Mrs. Dibble and often says: "You know, if you went over there quick and gave that rope a good yank, you could pull his head right off his body. What do you say we try it for laughs?"

I heard Mrs. Fuller say that Mr. Fuller won't take any kind of exercise. She says he sits and watches television and always identifies with the bad guys against the good guys. He sometimes watches the rest of us on our exercise machines, however, and says it always makes him feel better.

It's funny, none of the wives around here seem to need exercise. Green Eyes says it is because they stoop and reach and bend and fetch and carry all day long. All except Mrs. McMurty. She works as hard as the others, too, I guess, but she is a compensatory eater because she feels that Mr. McMurty doesn't really love her.

But the point I wanted to make is that the best time to exercise is when television is on. You can row *away* from it, or pedal *away* from it, or like my friend Mr. Blair, do your deep-knee bends during the commercials.

*   *   *

I used to be a do-it-yourself house repair guy myself until one day I bought a new ball for the flush tank in my upstairs bathroom, and I seated it and flushed the tank — and every other tank in every other bathroom on the street flushed at the same time. The thing was impossible, but it happened.

We had plumbers out, and the neighbors had plumbers out, and they asked me: "What in heaven's name did you *do*?" and I said: "All I did was take the old ball out and put this new ball in, and I adjusted it so it was properly seated, and then I flushed the tank to try out the new ball, and all the other fixtures in the neighborhood flushed at the same time. There is an interconnection and interdependence here of fixtures in this neighborhood, obviously, and you just can't say it is impossible because it is very much possible indeed."

A plumber would flush my fixture and then call another plumber in a house down the street, and he would say: "I just flushed the Welch fixture, Charlie. What happened where you are?" And the other plumber would say: "They just flushed here, too, both upstairs and downstairs."

People would be sitting watching television two blocks away, and their bathroom fixtures would suddenly flush for no reason, and they would tell one another: "Well, there goes Welch again."

But that's nothing like Dibble. He put in a new doorbell and the lights in the house next door went off. My lights, a block away, went *on*, with nobody in the house. Dibble was getting the juice for his doorbell off the house line and running it through a transformer that dropped it to twelve volts. He disconnected this power supply and put his doorbell on *batteries*, and still the lights around here all dim down when someone pushes Dibble's doorbell. Of course we live in a modern neighborhood, and I think they put some of these houses together pretty fast, and it could be that all our houses are still connected by some kind of umbilical cord.

When Mrs. Fuller sets her oven at 450, why Green Eyes' broiler here, a good 300 feet away in a straight line, goes off and the oven comes on. We had electricians out, both of us, and the only way we settled it is that both families have the same dishes every night, and dinner at the same time.

I forgot whether I told you about Hixly. His kitchen sewer line got clogged, and he rented one of these devices that bore through a sewer line on the end of a long flexible cable. He let out 100 feet of line and wondered when he was coming to the junction with the main sewer in the alley — and found he had bored right across the junction and into the sewer line up to the Jacks' kitchen. Mr. Jack's sewer line goes right under my house, and we heard this grinding noise under our basement floor, and Green Eyes said: "What's that?" And I said: "I don't know, and I am not going to worry about it, either. You are always hearing noises." And she said: "Well, it's moving." And I said: "Maybe it is a big mole." Grandma thought it was the Russians.

What about Honest Al Carter's and Mr. Leighton's radio devices in their cars that open and close their garage doors by remote control when they are arriving or leaving? As I understand it, they are different systems by different makers. But one day Mr. Leighton had Dorothy's new Juggernaut GT halfway out of the garage, polishing it, and Honest Al Carter came along and signaled to open his garage door across the alley, and Leighton's door came down on the hood of Dorothy's car and made one fine jolly dent in it. They had nineteen people out looking for the trouble, and all nineteen said it was impossible.

Honest Al Carter said it was Leighton's fault. Leighton installed his system himself to save money. So now when Honest Al Carter's door is down, Leighton's is up, all night long sometimes. And vice versa.

What happened to the Blairs and the McMurtys who live

side by side is not do-it-yourself but it shows the inter-dependence we all have upon one another. McMurty got a television set with a remote control to turn it on or off, change stations, and adjust the audio to loud or soft. The Blairs, next door, admired the set and got one, too.

Now when Mr. McMurty or the Blairs operate their remote control devices, both sets are affected. While the Blairs are looking at a sweet soap opera, McMurty will go into his den and try to find a ball game and switch the Blairs' show off during the prettiest part.

I came down from the bus stop the other evening and there was a power truck outside my house and several workmen standing around. Every house in the neighborhood seemed to be dark except mine, and I asked one of the line-men: "What's up?" And he said: "We don't know yet. But we think Grandma must have connected everything in her room all at the same time. The whole neighborhood is dark, and it blew out the power house again."

And I said: "Well, if it is like you say — if Grandma plugged in all her electrical appliances at the same moment, why isn't my house dark too?" And he said: "Nobody really knows much about electricity yet. We do know in a general way how it should perform, but it takes a genius to follow all those wires in Grandma's room."

I went right into the house and called Mr. Pritchard, the plumber. The foreman of the line crew said: "We don't need no plumber," and I said: "Mr. Pritchard is not just a plumber. He is a genius and he can fix pretty near anything." While we were waiting for Mr. Pritchard, we checked over Grandma's appliances.

Let's see, in her room she has an electric blanket, and an electric pad, a heater, a radio, a television set, an old-fashioned curling iron which fills the house with the odor of burned hair, an electric clock, three lamps, an electric steamer for stuffed-up sinuses; an electric sewing machine, and an electric toaster and a coffee percolator so that when she gets mad at us she can lock herself in her room and keep house.

Grandma swears she never has all these devices connected up at once, but there are times when the whole county blacks out, and I have even seen jet transports overhead black out when they were passing over my house, and their lights didn't come back on until they were some distance away.

I understand sometimes the jet pilots get on their public address system and say to the passengers: "This is your captain speaking. There is no reason for alarm. Welch's mother-in-law has connected all the electrical appliances in her room again, and it has blacked out most of the state, but they have an auxiliary system at the airport and they will get it working any minute now, I hope. Meanwhile the stewardesses will pass among you with lighted candles."

Well, Mr. Pritchard, the plumber and handyman, showed up pretty soon, and he went directly into the kitchen where Grandma was looking guilty, and he said in his sad way: "Now, what have you been doing, you naughty girl?" And Grandma said: "I was only running the sewing machine and television and the curling iron." And Mr. Pritchard said: "Have you by any chance overloaded the washing machine again?" And she said: "Of course not. I was only washing my bedroom rug."

Mr. Pritchard found the washing machine fuse blown, and he replaced it, and the lights came back on for miles around. We had to take the washing machine apart to get the rug out.

You would have thought Mr. Pritchard would be pleased to show how smart he is, but he seemed more morose than ever. The truth is he feels rejected by society. His first name is John and he takes it personally that so many women lightly call the bathroom fixture "John." Old Mrs. Wahlster, her first name is Babette, once telephoned Mr. Pritchard and thoughtlessly said: "John, will you come and fix our John," and Mr. Pritchard said: "How would you like it if someone called it a Babette?" and Mrs. Wahlster was mightily offended.

The lineman said admiringly to Mr. Pritchard: "Boy, you sure found the trouble here right away, all right." And Mr. Pritchard said: "Any time anything goes wrong in the neighborhood I come here first."

I only tell you this to show you how utterly interdependent the wiring and the plumbing and the water systems are in these new residential neighborhoods. The lights are back on now, but I understand the Blairs across the street still can't get their bathrooms to work and their front doorbell rings constantly.

*   *   *

I have been reading lately where American men are afraid they are not masculine, and how advertising people have been exploiting this uncertainty. I mean you turn on the TV and here is a commercial of a hairy type who talks as though he hadn't finished a sentence in his whole life and he is pushing a hay wagon uphill unassisted, or he is carrying a thousand-pound bull around on his shoulders, or he is lifting a house by one corner, or sometimes he is half-naked and oozing masculine sex appeal. And then he whips out a can of man-type anti-perspirant, or beer, and right away you realize that this anti-perspirant, or beer, is only used by genuine masculine types, and also that if you use it you are automatically a sexy man right there.

Psychologists say that most of us fellows are not sure we are authentic males and that's why we wear beards and boots and sea captains' caps and fishermen's sweaters under our dinner jackets.

Well, I look around this neighborhood of mine, and truly I don't find many men worrying about whether they are men. The young ones have one or two children (and often one on the way), and it never seems to occur to them that they are not men. And once in a while I hear their wives, the young ones, complain to Green Eyes that they are not only men but inconsiderate oppressors. And I hear the older wives say the same thing.

I often hear Mrs. McMurty say that her husband is an Old Goat, and that is a kind of left-handed way of saying that he is too much a man. She says this mostly when he has been paying some pretty compliment to The Widow who lives next door. Mr. McMurty will carry a martini out to The Widow who is standing in her yard and Mrs. McMurty will throw her window up and say: "What do you think you are doing *now*, you old goat!" In her mind there is no doubt that he is *all man*, and not to be trusted a minute.

I am pretty sure I am a man, too, but I do wear a commodore's cap, a yachtsman's cap, when I take a bath with my big red ferryboat and the two cruisers and the plastic ducks my grandchildren left behind. I said to Green Eyes the other night: "Do you think the fact that I wear a commodore's cap when I take a bath and run my big red ferryboat indicates an ambiguity in my male role?" And she said: "No, to me it means only that you have a bird on your head. You're a little ding-a-ling. I never worry when you take a bath with your commodore's cap because, after all, you *are* running your big red ferryboat in the bathtub. I won't worry until you start wearing one of *my* hats in the bathtub."

I called up Mr. Dibble, my neighbor down the block, to ask him if he was worried about being a man. And he said: "Wait a minute, Welch. I don't hear you too good. I just turned on the dishwasher. It was my turn to do the dishes tonight."

And I said: "Do you have to do any other housework?" And he said: "It's all written up here on the kitchen bulletin board. On Thursday I dust the living room. On Tuesdays I have to make the school lunches for the quick getaway Wednesday. The only thing I hate is the ironing. . . ."

Well, nobody can say Mr. Dibble is not a man. I guess he

is probably the greatest lady-pincher in this part of the country.

There is a kind of a rule of thumb and index finger around here that Mr. Dibble is entitled at parties to the first pinch all around, but then a lady will say: "Okay, you have had your pinch. Now the next time you try it I am going to bend your nose." There is no doubt among the ladies that he is masculine.

The only man I know who should worry whether he is male is young Mr. Starbright whom all the ladies around here are trying to marry off to The Widow. He is so *nice*. He is so polite. He sits and talks with the ladies while the rest of us are standing at the bar. I think The Widow has some reservations about his masculinity. I heard her say to him once: "Why don't you get good and mad about something once, and loud, even if you are unreasonably wrong?" And he said: "But, Lola, what is there to get mad about?" And she said: "If you thought about it long enough, you could always come up with something."

We all hoped that when Mrs. Peterson's husband came back briefly from the sea, why she would take a turn for the better. We thought she might stop thumbing her nose at Fred, the mailman, for not leaving her some mail. And we desperately hoped that she would stop accusing the President of reading her mail and listening in on her telephone conversations to her sister, Agnes, in South Dakota.

But the trouble is that Captain Peterson *believed* her! I have heard that some sea captains are among the most naive persons on land, and he sort of proves the point. He is a tiger on the bridge and the scourge of harbormasters all over the world. There was a time when he said to his wheelsman: "I want you to turn port two degrees. Right." And the wheelsman said: "Cap'n, port is left. Right is starboard." And Peterson looked him right in the eye and said: "Not on this ship, it isn't. It's whatever I say it is." You don't mess with him at sea, but he is a babe on land.

Well, he comes home and hears the President has been reading his wife's mail and listening to her phone calls and I try to persuade him that his wife is entertaining one big, fat fantasy, but he won't buy it. I even suggest a few lessons for her from Dr. Spook and he says no thanks, he is quite capable of taking care of Mrs. Peterson himself.

The next thing we know the captain has bugged his home with burglar alarms and electric eyes and I don't know what. The first day when Fred, the mailman, did go up on the porch with some mail, why the bell went off like the James boys were blasting into a bank in East Kansas. You see, Fred opened the screen door to put the mail out of reach of dogs and kids and an electrical contact was broken and the alarm sounded. The captain came running out and made a grab at Fred, but happily, The Widow was walking by and identified him.

Then the milkman set off the alarm on the back porch an hour later and the whole neighborhood turned out to spring him.

The captain himself came home late that same night and it sounded like a three-alarm fire. Mrs. Peterson had gone to bed and left everything on, including the hinged step on the way upstairs. When you step on it it swivels and you fall in a hole and break your leg — that's to hold you until the police come.

The captain didn't break his leg but he did bark his shin something awful, and when the police came — Mrs. Peterson called them when she heard all the bells — the captain ordered them out in the rough idiom of the sea and they did not care to be addressed in the rough idiom of the sea.

Well, the captain paid his fine and went off to sea again, and now every night a bell rings at Mrs. Peterson's house and we wonder if it is a cat or if the President is fooling around again.

* * *

Mr. Thorndyke who lives just north of the Dibbles invents things. I would say he's an engineer except that he isn't working at the moment. He *was* an engineer with an airplane company until one day they walked into his office and found that he had made a whole suit of chain mail out of paper clips.

Making the suit of chain mail out of paper clips wasn't so bad. I think what bothered his superiors was that he was *wearing* it at his desk. They decided he needed a rest, so they gave him early retirement and he has been spending most of his time since in his basement workshop inventing things.

I worry about Mr. Thorndyke quite a little because he seems to be regressing. Last year he was inventing running boards for automobiles, and before that he was inventing a whistle for steam locomotives, and he was also inventing a biplane which was really a big open kite, and the pilot sat out in the open in a sheepskin coat with helmet and goggles and pulled a couple of levers.

The biplane was the best of his inventions, I think, and the little model he made performed beautifully except that on the second flight it went into the Fullers' open bathroom window and hit Mrs. Fuller. The Fullers are very sensitive and apprehensive about their upstairs back bathroom, anyway, because Mr. Jack has his cannon trained on it.

The day the biplane model came through the bathroom window Mrs. Fuller had checked to make sure Mr. Jack was not fooling around with his cannon across the alley, and then — boom! — the airplane comes in.

Mr. Thorndyke's latest invention is a garlic spray in an aerosol can. I have been wondering for the last two months why he smelled like a two-dollar Italian table d'hote dinner. I mean, he gets on the bus, and it stops at the next block and everybody else gets off, including the driver.

Well, Green Eyes uncovered his secret one day when she was at the Thorndykes' collecting for the PTA missions overseas. Mrs. Thorndyke asked her to stay for tea and cake. The cake, a three-layer Devil's food, tasted strongly of garlic, and

Mrs. Thorndyke explained that her husband has invented this process of combining garlic with distilled water under pressure. You press a button and the device emits a fine garlic spray. The water evaporates but the garlic remains. A fine garlic mist hangs over the kitchen and permeates everything, including a lady's hairdo, but Mrs. Thorndyke explained that the device is still not completely perfected.

I feel very strongly that if there is anything we don't need in this world, it is a garlic spray. My distaste for garlic in any form dates back to high school. I was going with this girl — well actually, I was *running away* from her — who was a real double-whistle except that her father made her eat a fried-garlic sandwich before she went out on a date. It was his idea of protecting her from any misadventures, and I want to tell you, it worked. About the only way you could handle her was drive an open-top car. We had an agreement. She promised she would sit way over on her side — and dance with somebody else at the dance. She was gorgeous to look at, and she had this low, coaxing, sultry voice, but perfumed she was not.

For that matter, I was no bargain myself. I was the Fastest Pimple in the West in those days. We made a nice couple. Incidentally, she got married finally. A kid showed up her father liked, and the first night she went out without eating a garlic sandwich, she got engaged.

Thorndyke thinks there is a great market for garlic spray. A couple of whishes on a tossed salad before it comes to the table, a spurt on a chopped-liver sandwich — he believes it will be the greatest advance in gourmet cuisine since ketchup.

* * *

Our broker, Sam Insull, says you are not to worry about the stock market. So today the market is selling off. So tomorrow it goes up. He says all you have to do is live long enough.

Sam Insull, that name is familiar! I have this vague recollection of having seen pictures years ago of someone named Insull going in and out of criminal court with a newspaper shielding his face. I once asked Sam if his people were ever in the traction and interurban business around Chicago, and he said no, he had an uncle who once was a motorman on the old Chicago and South Shore, but the rest of his people mostly sold Edsels and before that Cords.

Sam has his office in the low-rent district, right next door to a wholesale poultry dealer, in fact. This is convenient because Sam keeps abreast of the market, and what it will do *tomorrow,* by studying the insides of chickens. The same way the old Roman augurs did. I mean you ask Sam when Gulf Oil is going to climb back to what you paid for it and he goes next door and buys a chicken and opens it up right on his desk before you and shows you what Gulf Oil is going to do a month from now.

Sam's clients know what is coming long before the clients of other brokers do. Sam calls them and says, "I have been getting spotted livers in all my chickens lately, and it tells me that international and domestic oils are in for a little trouble."

I say to Sam, "Well all right, suppose I sell now? I will have to pay a whopping big capital gains tax, and then I face the problem of where to put my money." And he says, "How about recreational land?" And I say, "What have you got available?" And he says, "For you, because you are a friend, I got a little acreage that is a sweetheart. Right on a highway and . . ."

And I say, "Right on a highway, eh?" And he says, "Well, not exactly a highway. It's more like a county road." And I say, "A county road, eh?" And he says, "Let me put it this way, the road isn't there yet but it's in the budget for the next year and it's near one of the biggest lakes in the state." And I say, "How near?" And he says, "A hundred and ten miles. These days, when everyone has his own plane, it's like living on the beach."

I mean you get honest, direct answers from Sam. I say to him, "Did you open up a chicken to study the prospects of this recreation land deal?" And he says, "That goes to show how little you understand the brokerage business. You don't study the inside of chickens to evaluate real estate! For real estate I got this wheel in my office I spin, and if it comes up an even number you got a winner there, fella!"

Once I said, "Sam, look, how about debentures? Maybe this would be the time to buy debentures." And his answer was significant. He said, "What are debentures?" I mean he doesn't pretend to know *everything*. He lowered his voice and said: "I've got a horse in the third at Santa Anita which is safer than government bonds. You interested in a piece of him?" And I said, "I'll take across the board." And he said, "Look, as your broker, I advise it right on the nose, to win." It won and paid $27.70 on a $2 ticket. While I was waiting for the results in his office I also won $12 at hooligan, so I cannot really say the market has been bad for me lately.

Sam does not claim that his market analysis system is infallible. He does admit that he gets better results out of White Leghorns than out of Plymouth Rocks. And he gets superb results from turkeys, but he only opens up a turkey for 100-share lots of blue chips. There was a time when he let you take the fowls home free, which was the only way some of his clients managed to eat. Now he has to charge retail. I can hear you saying, "Why not buy your chickens from the poultry dealer next door?" The answer is that the poultry dealer doesn't give you a market forecast along with the poultry. All you can say for the poultry dealer is that he wraps the birds a little neater. Sam just hands them to you in a large manila envelope.

I went to see him right after New Year's Day to get a new market forecast. Unhappily, Sam was hiding out somewhere. It seems that he booked a client's horse bet himself. He thought the chance of this horse coming in was decidedly remote, so he booked it himself, and the horse, a real pig, came in to win and pay about $62.50 on a $2.00 ticket.

The customer came around to pick up about two hundred bucks and Sam had to go out the side door through the poultry market. He raised the money somewhere and reappeared, and his latest prediction is that some stocks will go up this year and some stocks will go down. He also says that he expects "change," and I do believe this is about as accurately as *any* broker can dope the long-term market.

Sam has worked out a chart which is very helpful in making stock choices. It consists of the printed names of all the stocks on the New York and American exchanges and all listed in the Over-the-Counter market, printed to look like a donkey. You blindfold yourself and try to pin the tail on the donkey, and where the pin goes in, *that* is the stock to buy *right now!*

The beauty of the Educated Guide to Stock Purchasing — this donkey, I mean — is that when it is not being used by the man of the house to determine his purchases, it can be utilized as a game at children's birthday parties. Some kids have made small fortunes.

CHAPTER XVII

The Welches

Husbands of wives who don't have jobs wonder sometimes what goes on at home. I work a lot at home, and I can tell you right now what goes on. The telephone rings almost constantly and strange men who only have first names are walking in and out of the house all day as if they belonged.

The other day Green Eyes and Grandma were downtown and I went into the kitchen and a fellow is there opening up the kitchen closet door. "Who are you?" I said. And he said, "Hello, Mr. Welch. I am Joe." And I said, "Well Joe, can I help you?" And he said, "Oh no, I know where everything is." And I said, "What particularly are you looking for?" And he said, "Your laundry and cleaning. Mrs. Welch leaves it here for me." And I said, "You just walk in through the back hall and get it?" And he said, "Yeah, Mrs. Welch has a system. When she's not home she leaves the key and I come in and get it."

And I said, "You're better off than I am. If I forget my own key I have to wait at a neighbor's until she comes home. And he said, "Oh, she has a key cached away outside all the time. Do you want I should tell you where it is?" And he told me.

So a little later there is another male footstep in the kitchen and it is the milkman. He knows where the key is, too.

"I guess you must be the milkman," I said. And he said yes. He was Al. He was leaving two cartons of cottage cheese. I said, "I'd rather have the kind with the chives in it," and he said, "No, I don't think so. I think your missus is going to make cheesecake with this and chives would louse it up." And I said, "How could you possibly know she was going to make cheesecake?" And he said, "When she orders two cartons it is always for cheesecake." And I said, "Oh." He knows her better than I do.

The telephone rings and I answer, and a male voice says, heavy with suspicion, "Who is this?" And I say, "You tell me who you are and I'll tell you who I am." And the voice says "Are you *Mister* Welch?" And I say, "I might be and then again I might not be." And he says, "This is Chuck, the furnace man. I'll call later." And I say, "What can't you discuss now?" And he says, "Do you know whether you need a new filter when I come out to fix your furnace this afternoon?" And I say, "No, I don't know." And he says triumphantly, "Well, your wife *does* know and that's why I will call her before I come out."

The next time the telephone rings I pick it up and say, "Union Cab." And a woman's voice says, "Isn't this the Welch residence?" And I say, "Union Cab. Where to, ma'am?" and she hangs up. The phone rings again in a moment. It is the same lady. She's from Grandma's church. "I dialed your number a moment ago and somebody said, 'Union Cab,'" she announces. And I say, "You couldn't have dialed this number because this is the Welch residence and there wasn't anybody here a moment ago." And she said, "Well, I know I didn't make a mistake and somebody *did* say 'Union Cab.'"

And I say, "I am sorry, but I am too busy to listen to fantasies. Whom do you want at this number?" She wants to talk to Grandma. I say, "My mother-in-law and wife are downtown shopping. I'll take the message."

Grandma is to come to a meeting of the Altar Guild and it is at Mrs. Hempstead's house and you get on the No. 6 bus and get off at Trummer Street and turn right ... and I say, "Couldn't you possibly call Grandma when she is home, in about an hour or so?" No, she couldn't. She's got to go to the doctor and see about her knee. And Grandma is to bring a cake, and the meeting will be next Thursday at the Congregational Church.... And I say, "You have the wrong number. My mother-in-law belongs to a church where they knock on your front door and play a phonograph record when you open it." And she gasps and hangs up.

The next voice on the telephone wants no part of me. "Is the lady of the house in?" the voice, a young lady asks. And I say, "This is the lady of the house. I have a cold and I am hoarse." And she says, "I want to talk to Mrs. Welch." And I say, "Actually, I am a recording. But go ahead. Make your pitch." And she says, "I wonder if you would be interested in aluminum siding. We have a wonderful ..." And I say, "I am a recording. Good day."

The phone rings again and I say again, "Union Cab." It's the lady from the church with the knee. She says, "Ah, ha! I know it is you, Mr. Welch. You said 'Union Cab' to me the last time!" And I say, "The phone rings here so much I might just as well be dispatching cabs. ..."

Sometimes it takes Green Eyes days to straighten out the telephone calls. And a funny thing happened on the bus. A fellow said to me, "I hear your mother-in-law belongs to one of these groups that plays phonograph records against the Church." And I said, "I wouldn't be surprised. To the best of my knowledge she is a staunch Congregationalist, but she may be leading a double life. I wonder how a rumor like that ever gets started?"

Just the other day I am in the kitchen at home, waiting to turn the heat off under the chicken. Green Eyes said to be sure to turn it off at 4 P.M. The telephone rings. A lady with a real nice, sultry voice says, "Is the lady of the house in?"

And I said, "Well, you might say that I am the lady of the house at the moment." And she said, "I wanted to ask the lady of the house some questions." And I said, "Ask me. I know everything." And she said, "Do you do any of the family shopping?" And I said, "Certainly. And right now I am wearing an apron because I just did the breakfast dishes and lunch dishes and I am waiting to turn the chicken off at 4 P.M." And she said, "I wanted to ask some questions — this is a survey — of the lady of the house." And I said, "This would be difficult to do because the lady of the house is downtown with my mother-in-law spending my money. They have left me in charge here."

And the lady said, "What is this about turning the chicken off?" And I said, "We are having curried chicken for dinner. My wife started the chicken simmering and I turn it off. Then she comes home and thickens the chicken stock and adds Madras curry powder and, voila! we have curried chicken. Of course she serves it with raisins and shredded coconut and peanuts and green onions and rice and like that. About a five-boy curry." And the lady said, "It sounds heavenly. Do you do any of the cooking yourself?" And I said, "Only when they catch me." And the lady said, "Is your wife currently on a diet?" And I said, "She's always on a diet." And she said, "Would you say that your wife is underweight or overweight or average weight?" And I said, "She's just right. I used to be able to encircle her waist with my two hands when we were first married, but now I would need a third hand." And she said, "I'll put down that your wife is just right."

And I said, "Thank you so much. Am I on television or something? Do I get a prize?"

And she said, "Do you know how much Slim Kid your wife buys every month?" And I said, "No, but I see it around here sometimes." And she said, "Do you ever use Slim Kid yourself?" And I said, "No, I prefer booze. And then I don't eat. I find you can lose a pound a day on coffee and martinis and no food and it is a romp from breakfast to bedtime." And she said, "Oh, dear, I don't think I can put that answer down."

And I said, "Tell me about you. You sound kind of sexy."

And she said, "I am not allowed to. May I ask if your wife ever buys any competing slimming drinks?" And I said, "No, she doesn't because we have found that all the other slimming drinks make my mother-in-law's pores stick open. She has pore trouble. Her pores won't open and close like other people's pores. Sometimes they stick open and then electrical drafts get into them and give her arthritis. But Slim Kid doesn't seem to do this." And she said, "I don't know whether to believe you or not." And I said, "This very morning my mother-in-law said she believed your product helps close her pores when they stick open."

And she said, "Are you really wearing an apron?" And I said, "Yes, a plastic apron with rosebuds. When the milkman came an hour ago he was enchanted by it. He wanted to go steady with me." And she said, "It is four o'clock right now — if you really are supposed to turn off the chicken." And I said, "Thank you a heap. I am supposed to put it on 'warm.'" And the lady said, "I wish I had some more questions to ask you." And I said, "That's the nicest thing anyone ever said to me."

When Green Eyes came home she said, "Why the big stupid grin?"

And I said, "Oh, it is just that a very sexy lady called me up. She was crazy about me. She wanted to have an affair with me but I told her I didn't have time. I had to stay here and turn off the chicken. . . ."

And Green Eyes said, "Ha, that's rich, that is."

* * *

I met Green Eyes outside the dentist's office and kissed her and she said: "That's the sloppiest kiss you ever gave me," and I said: "My wips are still mumb fum the Novocain." And she said: "Well, at my age I am glad to be kissed by *anybody*."

Then we went to this restaurant and, mostly by signals, I ordered a martini. When it came I raised it to my face, but my lips didn't snap at it the way they usually do. Sometimes they rack out as far as an anteater's tongue to a martini. But this time they failed utterly to signal when the glass reached them, and I tilted the glass higher and higher, and the contents cascaded down my chin, my necktie and my jacket and puddled in my lap. Every last drop.

Green Eyes said: "Well, it is a little hard on your clothes, but if you *must* drink martinis, that certainly is the way to do it. I wouldn't worry a minute about you if you drank them all that way."

So the waitress came and Green Eyes ordered another for me, and asked the waitress: "Bring a straw with the next one." And the waitress said: "A straw? A straw to drink a martini?" And Green Eyes said: "Of course."

People all over the room turned and regarded me with astonishment as I sipped the second martini through a straw and carried the olive up to my mouth with both hands, and a fellow at the next table said to his wife in a stage whisper: "When they get that bad, they shouldn't be allowed any booze at all."

Well, unfortunately Mrs. McMurty witnessed this incident. She is a natural-born stool pigeon.

She came over to the table and said: "Heavy weather, I see." And Green Eyes said: "I don't like to disappoint you, but he has been to the dentist and the Novocain made his lips numb and he is not able to drink any kind of liquid at the moment."

And Mrs. McMurty said: "I know, I know. It happens to my husband two, three times a week, when he has been drinking since middle-afternoon."

I went back to see the dentist. Actually he is putting in a couple of wisdom teeth for me. Also I wanted to see how he was because last session I bit down pretty hard but I understand they will be able to save his thumb. He said if you think it is funny to watch a fellow drink when his lips have lost their feeling, you ought to see women trying to put on their lipstick. He says he has to put it on for them.

He says he can do the most marvelous job with lipstick, makes the finest cupid bow anywhere. He says they ought to give a quick course in this in dental school. And I said: "Do you always make women remove their lipstick before you work on them?" and he said: "I certainly do. Do I want to go home with lipstick on my finger and maybe on the collar of my shirt?"

Well, it just goes to show you. You learn something every day.

*   *   *

We were on the road again and Green Eyes said: "Would you be a prince of a fellow and stop at the next gas station?" And I said: "You're kidding." And she said: "What's to kid?"

And I said: "For heaven's sake, we are not yet out of sight of the last gas station. I can still see it in my rearview mirror." And she said: "Well, here we go again." And I said: "I filled up at the last place. There's no room in the tank for more." And she said: "We must have used up a gallon or two." And I said: "I am not going to wheel up and ask for two gallons of gas. I am not a teen-ager, you know."

And she said: "You stop outside and I'll run in." And I said: "Oh, no. The guy that runs the place hates me because you are using his facilities and I am not buying anything." And she said: "So buy a pint of oil." And I said: "I changed my oil yesterday, don't you remember, the tenth time we stopped."

And she said: "Oh don't be ridiculous. If it is going to embarrass you, buy some more windshield cleaner." And I said: "We've already got a case of it on the back seat." And she said: "Get a soft drink." And I said: "I'm floating in it, and the profit on a soft drink doesn't pay the guy for the time it takes to hand you the key." And she said: "It's a big company. Losses on one station average out with profits on the next." And I said: "These are independent operators. They get no part of the profits of other stations." And she said: "You would think a big company like that would have a more reasonable arrangement."

And I said: "They didn't know about you. I'm trying to tell you there is no profit in facilities. The fellow doesn't go home at night and tell his wife, 'I didn't pump much gas today, but, man, what a business I did with facilities!'" And she said: "Don't take that superior attitude toward me. All I want is to stop at the next gas station." And I said: "Your trouble is that you don't plan ahead. You don't organize. Now look at me. I plan." And she said, "Oh, shut up."

And I said: "I am lucky Grandma is not with us. She doesn't use the facilities when you do. She waits until the next. We make one hundred miles a day and stop at ninety-two gas stations." And she said: "Oh, really!" And I said: "Other fellows make four, five hundred miles a day, with only one lunch and gas and facility break." And she said: "Those gas station men don't think anything of it at all." And I said: "The last time I stopped at the curb and you walked in I saw the fellow looking at me and he was talking to another fellow and I could see the words 'cheap ratfink' forming on his lips."

And she said: "Here is a station." And I said: "Thank heaven they have a restaurant with it. Whether we like it or not, we're going to eat lunch at 10:30 A.M." And she said: "There, you see? Your big crisis has dissolved again into nothing." And I said: "A bachelor would be two hundred miles further down the road."

*   *   *

There is a great deal to be said for the old custom of belling a woman. Women wore bells on their fingers and bells on their toes — actually on their shoes — and you always knew where they were in a house, and approximately what they were doing.

A fellow would be sitting in his living room or, as in my

case, in his "office," and he would hear bells which would tell him his wife was working in the kitchen, or making beds upstairs, or doing laundry in the basement, or mowing the lawn (I suppose in those days the women used scythes). And when the bell-ringing stopped, a fellow would know his wife was dogging it and had stopped working to sit down to a cup of tea, perhaps, and he would investigate and get her started working again.

A fellow would say to a friend: "Just help yourself to another drink, Wolfgang, while I investigate this silence. I don't hear my wife's bells." And the friend would say: "But I still hear bells." And you would say: "Her feet bells, yes. But not her hand bells. I know her feet are moving but what about her hands? She might be sitting down somewhere moving her feet to allay my suspicions."

I often wish I could bell Green Eyes because I never know where to find her when I can't spell a word. Most of the time I can't even come close enough to the spelling of a word to find it in the dictionary. So then I have to holler. And often she will sit in the kitchen and pretend she doesn't hear me. She has some odd notion that I should go to her when I want a word spelled, rather than call *her* to *me*.

Sometimes, though, she will come halfway to the kitchen door when I am shouting down from the top of the stairs, and she will say: "What *now,* my fat prince?" I am not fat any more, and I don't like the way she says "Prince."

I tried a cowbell once, but it didn't work out very well. She developed an astonishing insensitivity to cowbells almost from the first day. "I will ring this cowbell when I need you to spell for me," I said, "and you will be able to hear me anywhere in the house, even if you are outside talking over the hedge. And she said, I thought coldly: "Ring the bell and see what happens." What happened was nothing.

So then I found an old-fashioned silver table bell with which hostesses used to tinkle for their maids at dinner — hey, remember *those* days? — and that didn't work any better.

Then I found a police whistle Green Eyes used years ago to call the children, and we worked out a schedule where I blew it once for Grandma to come, and twice for Green Eyes to come. I blew myself red. Nothing. I would say, "Didn't you hear my whistle, for heaven sake?" And one or the other of them would look astonished and say: "What whistle is that?" or "Were you blowing the whistle?"

So now I have a bell system in the house with a button on each floor. It sounds like a fire house. We have three telephones, but it seems to me I answer every call at my desk. So when the call is for Green Eyes or Grandma, I press their signal — and they'll respond if they've heard the telephone ring, but they won't respond if I only want to know how to spell. I am sorry we men ever gave women the vote.

When a call comes for Grandma and I have pressed her signal, I have to wait and listen until I have heard her reply on another telephone before I hang up. And sometimes when she is slow to answer, I put the telephone down and continue with my work, so I hear things like: "Who was that man who answered?" And Grandma will say: "Oh, that's my son-in-law." And another woman's voice will say, heavily freighted with suspicion: "What's he doing at home at this time of day? Why doesn't he go downtown to work? I wouldn't put up with it for a minute."

Now I am back, full circle, to hollering again when I want a word spelled. I have found that Green Eyes *will* respond if I manage to suggest physical pain in my hollering. An age-old mothering instinct, I guess.

*   *   *

I wish I could say that I was well. The truth is, I don't feel so good. I don't talk about it much because people refuse to take my complaint seriously. They just laugh. My trouble is that I have this wandering umbilicus. It is a good two inches off center, and when I walk down the street I walk in one direction and my umbilicus points in another. It wouldn't bother a lot of people, but I'm *tidy*. It doesn't hurt or anything like that. But it poses a constant psychological hurdle.

I mean I sit on the bus and study the other passengers and they seem to be content, and I am sure their umbilici point in the same direction that the bus is going, but unless I sit at an awkward angle my umbilicus points out the window!

It is no consolation to read the medical literature and discover that many, many people have off-center navels and have never noticed it. I wish now I had never made tests on myself when I first heard about it. I went to the hardware store and got a plumb bob and a line. And the clerk said how big a plumb bob did I want, and how long a line. And I said I wanted a line long enough to drop from my nose to the floor because I wanted to see if my navel was off center, and the clerk said: "I have been in this hardware business thirty-five years, and now at last I have heard everything."

I went home, and we have this full-length mirror on the bathroom door, and I stood there with the plumb bob, and Green Eyes knocked on the door and said: "What are you doing in there? Let me in." And I said: "Gee, the minute a guy gets married he just waves goodbye to all privacy." And she said: "What on earth are you doing?" And I said: "Well, I will tell you, Nosy. I am determining whether my navel is off center, and I will tell you further that this plumb bob and line tells me that I am a very sick man."

She only burst into laughter with slapping her thigh and rolling in the aisles. My navel was a good one and a half inches off center *then* — it is now two inches unless I squinch it starboard — but I got no sympathy from *her*, let me tell you. She laughed all through dinner.

And that night we went to a show which was pretty dreary, and she sat in her seat and laughed — she was actually thinking about me and my dreadful plight — and people around her said to one another: "She must be at a different show than we are."

I was the first one in the doctor's office the next day, and he said: "They said there was an emergency." And I said: "I want a pill or something that will cure a wandering navel," and he said: "Oh, that. Everybody's navel is off center." And I said: "It is all right for you to treat it so lightly but I am compulsively neat and orderly, and I like things to be in their proper place."

So he taped me up, and gave me some directions for abdominal exercises, and I walked out of his office sideways, like a dog going down the street. The exercises helped for a while. You can do them while you are waiting for a bus, or while you are talking to your boss, or anywhere. Of course, sometimes people say: "You seem to be preoccupied with something else while I am talking to you." And then you say: "Well, you see I am contracting and letting go of my abdominal muscles because I have this navel which is off center and I am trying to bring it back into line. . . ." And then they laugh, I can't figure why.

Well, I was going by a trick and puzzle store one day, and I saw an artificial paste-on navel in the window for wearing with bathing trunks. You tape up your real navel and wear this artificial one way over on the side, and you get laughs on the beach, particularly if you wear it in back. I was thinking of trying this but it occurred to me it would be a real frightening thing to undress at night and look in the mirror and see *two* navels. Anyway, it would only have been a stopgap. It would have done nothing toward resolving my basic problem.

Dr. Spook, our neighborhood psychiatrist, told me some of his patients have no navels at all, which is, of course, the ultimate rejection of Mother. My own doctor, and he's no help either, says I have thrown my whole body out of balance by years of lifting drinks in my right hand, and that the drifting navel is one of the natural hazards of double-martini-drinking.

CHAPTER XVIII

The Holidays

I have been collecting personal accounts of all the space ships and other unidentified foreign objects which were seen during the Christmas and New Year holidays over my own peculiar neighborhood, and I believe I am now ready to report.

Mr. Dibble, who spent early New Year's morning on a sofa in a friend's house — they were afraid to move him; they were afraid he would spill — finally arose and made it home about 5 A.M. He hammered on his front door, his wife wouldn't let him in, and it was during this period when he made the most sensational sighting of all.

He said a space ship came down the street and slowed outside his home, backed up, and stopped. He said two blue-uniformed space men wearing silver stars came up on his porch and asked what he was doing, and he replied don't be silly, what did it look like? He was trying to get into his home so he could go to bed. They asked him if he was certain this was his home, and he said of course he was certain it was his home. He said it was where his wife and children lived, so that made it his home, didn't it? He said it was also where his mother-in-law lived.

The space men had a whispered conference and then one of them rapped loudly against the front door with what

Dibble described as a "magic wand" very much like a policeman's nightstick. A window flew up immediately overhead and Mr. Dibble's mother-in-law looked out. She used to own a carnival so she shouted: "Hey, Rube!" and she looked down at the blue-uniformed travelers from outer space and said: "What do you town clowns want here at this time of night?"

And one of the space men said to her: "Does this here character belong to you?" And she said: "He certainly doesn't belong to me, but he does belong to my daughter. She's soft in the head." And the space man said: "Well, come down and let him in." And she said: "That will be the day," and she closed the window.

The space man then beat on the door with his wand until Mrs. Dibble responded. She was very much put out with Mr. Dibble and she was not the least impressed by the space men. "I left him hours ago on a sofa down the street," she said, "and if he prefers to start keeping house on somebody's sofa rather than continue to live with me, I can't see that it is any of your business."

And one of the space men said: "Kindly take him in and shut the door or we will have to prefer charges against both of you for creating a disturbance, and we do not wish to do this." And Mr. Dibble said to Mrs. Dibble: "These two men are from a far-off planet and they have come to my succor and I believe the least we can do is offer them a cuppa coffee or a drink or something," and Mrs. Dibble said: "They are doing me no favor," and she let him in and shut the door in their faces.

Dibble says the space men then got into their space ship and flew away. He remembers distinctly the space ship carried a flashing red light on its roof.

Earlier the same morning Mr. McMurty also sighted this same space ship, a consequence of his trying to put his car away in a single-car garage already occupied by Mrs. McMurty's car. Mr. McMurty drove about twenty-seven feet on his own driveway into the back of Mrs. McMurty's car with a very satisfying crash just as the space ship cruised by, and it stopped and the same two space men got out and addressed Mr. McMurty.

"How far have you been driving, there, fella?" the space men asked, and Mr. McMurty said: "The length of my own driveway." And one of the space men put up the hood of Mr. McMurty's car and felt the motor and said, "It's cold, he's telling the truth." And the other space man said: "Whose car did you ram here?" And Mr. McMurty said: "My wife fondly believes it is *her* car but the registration is in my name." And the space man said: "You can't get two cars into a single-car garage, fella." And Mr. McMurty said: "You never know until you try." And the space men said: "You had better turn in there, fella," and Mr. McMurty did.

Quite a few of my neighbors also sighted our big steel multiple-legged community watertank ambling through the neighborhood. It often does this. It pulls itself right off its concrete foundations and pads around people's houses peering into bedroom windows. Mr. Blair saw it skittering across the boulevard as he and Mrs. Blair were going home (she didn't see it), and Mr. Fuller said he saw it stepping gingerly over Mr. Jack's house as he went to the refrigerator to get a final can of beer for the night. He was studying it through the kitchen window when Mrs. Fuller shouted: "Are you *ever* coming to bed?" and Mr. Fuller said: "That water-tank is running around again and some day it is going to sit on somebody's house and squash every living thing in it." And Mrs. Fuller said: "Don't come to me for sympathy tomorrow." She didn't even bother to look out the bedroom window.

I am sending all this data to the Air Force for its UFO files, although in the case of the watertank it really isn't Unidentified. We know what the nasty thing is.

* * *

The Crabgrass is beginning to green up in our lawns and Hixly still has a Santa Claus in his front window, and the whole neighborhood is disturbed because we think it is lowering our property values.

This Santa Claus is animated and life-size and flood-lighted. Furthermore it stands right inside his view window, looking outward at the street, and it waves to passing motorists. It also waves when nobody is going by.

I think Hixly is enthralled by it. He made it himself and he somehow connected up a motor with a mechanism which raises the right arm. I have counted the number of times this Santa Claus waves in any given moment, and it is ten.

It was all right during Christmas. People would drive by in their automobiles and exclaim: "Oh, how clever!" and they would say to their kids: "Look, there is Santa, waving at you!" and the kids would say: "Personally, I think it is cornball." Truth from the mouths of little children.

The eyes are lighted and roll, too. Every time you look out your window across the street at the Hixly home, you see Santa waving his arm and rolling his eyes. I take pills for it but they don't do any good. Pills won't make it go away.

The Coopers, also on my side of the street, have developed tics. Cooper declines his head to the left in exact timing with Hixly's waving Santa Claus's arm. He has talked to Dr. Spook about it and Dr. Spook says, "Stop looking out the window." And Cooper says: "But this is America, and I have a right to look out my own window." And Dr. Spook says: "Yes, this is America, and Mr. Hixly also has a right to have a waving Santa Claus in his front window in the middle of March. But I am not sure being an American entitles him to have a Santa Claus whose eyes light up and roll."

Mr. Cooper's head nods in time to Hixly's Santa's arm, and Mrs. Cooper's eyes roll. Her eyes are busier than a chaperone's at the graduation dance at a home for delinquent girls. It is only when she has a couple of glasses of Muscatel that the rolling stops and her eyes fall into focus. If Hixly doesn't take his Santa Claus down pretty quick, she'll be an alcoholic.

The whole neighborhood is worried because, you see, Hixly traditionally never throws out his Christmas tree until late November of the next year. He throws it under the basement stairs along about February and lets it dry and season with the idea of chopping it up for his fireplace. But he never chops it up. Actually he doesn't throw it out for the garbage man to carry away until a new tree comes into the house. The garbage man is always astonished to find an old Christmas tree beside the cans three or four days *before* Christmas.

If Hixly leaves his waving Santa up until June or July — which is entirely possible unless one of us sets his house on fire — our property values here will be nil. Imagine trying to sell a house, and you've got the people almost hooked, and they look across the street in May or June and see a waving

Santa Claus in a view window. "Leave me out of here!" they will say. "I don't want to live across the street from a fellow who has a bird on his head."

Mrs. Hixly is no help. She says it is no use to talk to her husband about his waving Santa Claus because it will only make him more determined than ever not to take it down. You don't go pushing *him* around, let me tell you. McMurty says the only solution he sees to Hixly's Santa Claus is to hire some small kid from another neighborhood to walk by and let go with a brick.

The Bazettis had a tasteful Santa Claus in their Christmas scene. They had him floodlighted, on the roof, dropping down into the chimney. Actually it wasn't a "him," it was a girl Santa Claus with a pretty tight-fitting red blouse and a terrific build, and it attracted more passing motorists than Mr. Hixly's. Fellows would say: "Now *there* is a Santa Claus I would wait up for!" and their wives would say: "Oh, for heaven sake, Charlie, and in front of the children, too!"

Bazetti won the prize for the best-decorated house in the neighborhood and I wouldn't be surprised if Hixly's refusing to take *his* Santa down is retaliation or something. I may paint my own windows black.